The Gambler, His Wife and His God

By Donna Rogers

All Scripture quotations unless otherwise indicated are taken from The Holy Bible. New International Version Life Application Study Bible Copyright 2011 by Zondervan publisher.

Women Who Love Too Much. Robin Norwood Arrow/Orion Spring. Bluebird Ltd 2022

The Jesus I Never Knew Philip Yancey.
Zondervan New Ed edition 1 Feb 2002

CONTENTS

Dedication

Foreword

Part One - NICK

Chapter One   Beginnings

Chapter Two   Sent to Coventry

Chapter Three   Homeless

Chapter Four   God, Gasoline and Gamblers' Anonymous

Part Two - DONNA

Chapter Five   Beginnings

Chapter Six   A New Millenium

Chapter Seven   Paris

Part Three - NICK AND DONNA

Chapter Eight   After Paris

Chapter Nine   Two weddings and a lunch

Chapter Ten   We nearly didn't get married!

Chapter Eleven   Married at last

Chapter Twelve   Nick: 2003

Chapter Thirteen   Donna: 2003

Chapter Fourteen   Nick: 2004

Chapter Fifteen   Donna: 2004

Chapter Sixteen   The Jericho Project

Glossary of terms

Signs of problem gambling

Organisations and Contact information

About the Author

DEDICATION

If you are a problem gambler, or in a relationship with someone whose gambling is a problem for you or your family, I dedicate this book to you. It is my desire that you find help and hope between the pages.

Special thanks to my dear friend Helen for her inspiration, her patience and her guidance and without whom this book may never have been written.

To Catherine Brown editor and author coach at Transparent Publishing for all her help and support in the writing and editing of this book.

To Laura Murray at Peanut Designs for her advice and help in putting this book together.

Thanks to Helen Tilling for all her help advice and encouragement. To Nick, who I love so very much … and especially to Jesus … who brought us together.

FOREWORD

Addiction can be an open, or hidden, struggle for many families. There are many types of addiction, but this book is about the addiction of gambling. For the gambler, breaking free from the life they find themselves in often feels impossible. This is the story of a gambler and his wife.With the upsurge in opportunities for gambling, especially online, this is a timely book. Type the word "gambling" into your browser, and you are presented with colourful, stimulating advertisements. Both television and internet sites show smiling faces - the faces of winners. Many sites have welcome bonuses for new customers. It looks so easy … just a bit of fun … at first. In the Gambling Act 2005, gambling is defined as: betting, gaming or participating in a lottery. Definitions of the word refer to 'taking risks in the hope of desired results.' This book is an encounter with two people who have faced the gritty reality of addiction. What makes it different from many other books about gambling is that it is written from both points of view – the addicted, and the one faced with loving and supporting that individual. Their accounts appeal both to those desperately wanting release from their addiction, and to those family and friends dealing with the inevitable suffering this can often lead to. With the strength of the God they came to know, Nick and Donna Rogers fought through tofreedom from that addiction. This is not a triumphalist book, but a demonstration of the growing search for answers in a dark world. We see the paths that took them to the point of meeting and what happened to them from there on in. For any who face addiction, either personal or familial, and know the devastation it can cause to the individual's wider circle, this is a must read. This highly personal story of two people describes a life path that features family breakdown and financial ruin. They have written candidly about their experiences. It is also the story of a man and woman who kept faith with each other by God's grace. These are openly human experiences shared in the raw with us. In their present frontline ministry, they run a community café that supports people with addictions of various kinds, and those struggling with emotional, financial and mental health issues. It brings community together and provides a safe place for all ages. They continue to walk determinedly where they believe God wants them to be. It has been my privilege to be their friend, and to observe the development of this book.

Helen Copestake

~

I believe both Nick's story and Donna's, are profound and must be told. There are too many families suffering through gambling addiction, and too few resources that give the level of insight that Nick and Donna courageously do, through "The Gambler, His Wife and His God". It is both inspiring and informative.

I believe it will help innumerable people facing the same struggles. Empathy is a powerful motivator, and this book gives unparalleled access to Donna's journey, her health issues and marriage to Nick, the pain and suffering in the gambling addiction, and the ultimate victory and overcoming as a couple and as a family. It is a unique book, that is timeless in content and immeasurable in the positive impact it can bring to many individuals and families today.

Catherine Brown Editor and Author Coach, Transparent Publishing.

This is our story...

In many ways our early years were very different, by the time we met our lives contained more similarities than differences. The one thing that both of us had more than enough personal experience of, was addiction and its consequences.

Nick & Donna Rogers

PART ONE

NICK

CHAPTER ONE

Beginnings

I grew up in Coventry in the 1960s. Ours was a comfortable, middle-class family: two kids, a semi-detached house, and a car in the drive. Dad was a senior manager with the old Post Office, on the telephone side. Mum was a full-time housewife, and mother to me and my older brother. It sounds like the perfect family, which is the exact impression Mum and Dad wanted to give to people.

Much of my childhood was spent with my brother who had a childhood illness I often had to chaperone him to make sure he was ok. This was a huge responsibility for me as I was three years younger than him. Where he went, I went, his friends became my friends. Lifelong Coventry City Football supporters, we would go to Highfield Road and to away matches during the season. It was a ritual every weekend. We would get up Saturday morning and get ready to go to the match. My Mum and Dad were season ticket holders and never missed a game. If we were playing away from Coventry, we would take the football special. The club always chartered trains and coaches to take fans all over the country. They would be crowded, there would be singing and banter, and inevitably, 'bingo'. I remember the first time I played bingo I won! It paid for the whole day out. Whilst I never got hooked on the game, it was good to join in if we were travelling by train or coach.

We would often go to Gran's, she lived near Finham in Coventry. Gran was a no-nonsense Yorkshire woman. My brother Simon was clearly her favourite. She used to call us 'Number One' and 'Number Two.' It was many years later I would realise how that simple label had affected me. Her house was a large Victorian terrace situated close to the train line. It was quite dark and gloomy inside, with heavy brown furniture. A shelf ran around the walls filled with dozens of Toby jugs, and a huge, dark oak dresser was covered in blue Wedgwood plates and vases, and lots of silver candlesticks. In the dining room, on a similar dresser, she kept lots of old clay and wooden pipes. The house used to smell strongly of tobacco, even though Gran didn't smoke and the pipes had not been used for years. Heavy, bottle-green velvet curtains at the windows gave the house a gloomy, closed-in feel, not unlike a casino. The back room had a large oak dining table on which we played games, especially cards, such as Pontoon, Newmarket, and and the occasional game of Dominoes.

Gambling with Gran

Gran was the first person in her circle of friends to buy a colour TV. She bought it so that she could distinguish the 'colours' of the riders when she watched the horse racing. Gran was keen on most sports, including snooker, so the 'telly' came in handy. She held an account with Coral bookmakers, so we would watch the races, and Gran would credit her account with the winnings. On those occasions, she would make big, thick-cut chips cooked in beef dripping, served on bread spread generously with best butter, and lots of salt and vinegar. She wasn't the best of cooks. Her specialities were chips, fish fingers, pork chops, and baked beans. She also made fried scallops, which she called 'smacks', and the most wonderful Yorkshire puddings. But it was her chips we liked best. We would often go to her house with our friends, hungry after a day at school. Gambling with Gran became a regular event. We would place our bets and settle down to a game of cards, or the horse racing, our fingers and mouths greasy from the buttery chip batches.

My brother really enjoyed gambling, especially on the greyhounds. I would go along to keep him company. I didn't particularly enjoy the dogs at first, we used to always stay inside and watch the races from inside the grandstand wherever the was a bar and restaurant. For some reason, one night I made my way outside. The bookies on the pegs shouted to each other, signing with Tic Tac. Thousands of pounds were changing hands, the smell of the sand, and the disinfectant used to clean the dogs' paws after the race, were intoxicating to me.

The sound of the dogs barking, and the bright lights around the stadium gave the whole place a magical atmosphere; the noise and the buzz excited me. From that moment, I was well and truly hooked. It was like the first shot of heroin to a junkie. The greyhounds, along with the football, became my preferred pastimes, and where I won, and lost, the most money.

Looking back, the gambling started at an early age. We would play a game at school which entailed throwing coins at the school wall. Whoever got the nearest, pocketed all the cash. I was quite good at it. At home, I would play table tennis in the garage with my brother and we would bet against each other. The bets were fictitious, in so far as no money changed hands, but I was burdened by the fact that my brother kept a record of my losses, along with a tally of how much I owed him. I lived in fear of the day he would tell me to pay up.Academically average at school, I excelled at sport. Finham Park was a brand-new secondary modern, specialising in sport. I loved it. Football and cricket were my favourites, with golf ranking a close third. I played as a goalkeeper for my school, city and county. Eventually, I was scouted by Coventry City Football Club, which was in the top flight at the time. I had trials for Coventry and remember on the day in question Jimmy Hill was present. Still quite small for my age back then, I remember I spent the whole trial picking the ball out of the back of the net.

Disaster struck soon after. I developed a strange growth on the little toe of my left foot. At first it was sore, as though my shoe was rubbing it, then it grew and grew until it was the same size as my big toe. The bone had overgrown and it was really painful. I couldn't wear shoes or football boots. The consultant looked at it and shook his head; the only option was to have it surgically removed. I was laid up for some time to allow it to heal. After I recovered, I continued to play for school and city, and trained with AP Leamington and Coventry Sporting Club's youth teams. I was only fifteen at the time. Eventually, I was asked to play for a team which was invited to go to Belgium to play in a tournament there. It was my first trip abroad. All the other lads in the team were over eighteen. I was still at school but because I played open age football, I was allowed to play for them.

Blankenburg and a Bride-to-Be

It was on that trip I discovered I suffered from sea-sickness. Once on firm ground, the coach swallowed up the miles to Blankenburg, where we stayed in a small hotel. I should have been sharing a room with two other lads, but they got friendly with two girls, early on, so I didn't see them again for a few nights. I had the room to myself, which was fine by me. We stayed there for a week but actually only played for three days, which gave us lots of free time. We played hard and partied harder. I loved it.

Away from the 'eagle eyes' of my parents, I was enjoying my first taste of freedom. So much so, it was there I met the girl who was to become my first wife. She was the same age as me and came from Salford. We met in a club, both of us clearly underage, and then met up every night after that. On returning home, I would work in the Coventry Provident Building Society during the week, and at weekends I would travel up to Salford on the coach, as often as I could. Salford was a very different place back then. Gambling and drinking were common pastimes, and mainly male activities, apart from at the weekends when women would generally accompany their boyfriends and husbands. I was in my element and soon started to fit right in. I told my parents I wanted to leave home to live with my girlfriend's parents. They were horrified. Their image of Salford had been formed by watching episodes of Coronation Street. They did everything they could to stop me, they asked their friends to speak to me, and even the local vicar was drafted in. That backfired, because, having listened to my side of the story he encouraged me to go! Had my parents not been so against my leaving, things may have been very different. All their efforts succeeded in doing was to push me further away from them. It was the first time I had really rebelled against them and what a rebellion it turned out to be. Resigning from my job, I packed my bags and boarded a train heading north. I was just seventeen. The gambling began in earnest soon after I arrived. I found work in Manchester with an American bank. At first it was all exciting and new. I loved working in the city, but life in Salford was proving to be very unpredictable. My girlfriend's father was well known there, and I gained an unearned respect from people I hardly knew because I was related to him. Most lunch times I visited the bookies.

At weekends, the pubs and clubs in Bolton beckoned. Life was good.

Close Shaves

We were married in 1980 at Salford Cathedral and moved into a terraced house close to the in-laws. Our first son was born a year later. Soon after, our second son was born at only twenty-eight weeks. He weighed a pound and fitted easily into the palm of my hand. He was so fragile, with tubes and monitors all around him. I was scared to death of this little life lying in the incubator, terrified that he might die or be brain damaged. We had some sleepless nights, willing him to pull through.

He was the smallest, and youngest, baby to survive at that time. A national newspaper and local press soon got in touch, and pictures of us and our "miracle baby" were plastered all over the papers. It is testament to the amazing skill of the doctors and nurses who cared for him, that he grew up to be a normal young boy. He is now in his thirties with a child of his own.

As if this wasn't enough pressure to deal with, during this time, the bank I worked for started to make people redundant. I was last in, and therefore, first out. I couldn't cope with trying to take care of my young son, visiting the hospital most days to visit our newborn, alongside the knowledge I no longer had a job. My nerves were jangling, every day I was afraid of being found out. There was, however, some light on the horizon. Despite having only worked for the bank for two years, I received an extremely generous redundancy payment of over three thousand pounds.

It was a small fortune at the time. Over the next month, I would drop my oldest son at his grandparents' house and then set off to the bookies. I didn't dare tell them I had lost my job. By the end of the month, I had gambled away almost all the redundancy money. Feeling physically sick, I knew I would have to 'fess up' and tell them the truth; I couldn't sleep and lived in fear of anyone finding out. In desperation I bet my last fifty pounds on two horses. Both needed to win, to collect. The horses came in, and gradually, over a few days, I won back every penny I had lost. The relief was massive, it was nothing short of a miracle. My secret was safe, no need to worry my wife because things were going to get better. Our baby boy was gaining weight and would soon be discharged home. At the same time, the bank managed to find me a job with one of their customers, a huge textile importer. I told my wife about the redundancy, and softened the blow with the redundancy money and the promise of a new job. That should have been my wake-up call right there but, all it did was enable me to continue to gamble. I had my 'get out of jail free' card and was set up for a brand-new start. The new job lasted a matter of months. I continued to gamble massively, which affected my performance at work. I was called into the company secretary's office; I had screwed up some foreign exchange transactions I was asked to leave with immediate effect.

I was always chasing the next big win that would secure us financially. In truth, every win just made me more reckless. I started betting in thousands of pounds instead of hundreds. It may sound strange, but the money didn't really matter to me. It was merely ammunition to keep on gambling.

As a result, there were many close shaves during the gambling years. I used to hide money and betting slips all over the place. The problem was, I used to forget where I had hidden them. My favourite places were behind the skirting boards, on top of kitchen units or wardrobes, inside loft doors, and under carpets. Unbelievably, the first time I won 'big' our house was robbed. On that occasion, I had hidden the money in the false ceilings in the kitchen. The thieves lifted all the carpets, turned the mattresses over and emptied every drawer. Thankfully they didn't find the money, but it made me more aware that people were watching me.

Around that time, on my brother's recommendation, I backed a greyhound called 'Desert Pilot' to win in the English Greyhound Derby. I had backed it 'ante-post' at a number of different bookies and stood to win a large four-figure sum. By the time the day of the race came around I had forgotten which bookies I had laid my bets with, and went in search of the betting slips. I searched everywhere, becoming more and more frantic. Then I remembered; I had hidden them under the insoles of my shoes. Ecstatic that I had finally remembered where they were I went in search of the shoes. Lifting the insoles, to my horror, I found a congealed mess, the sweat from my festering feet had caused all the slips to weld together. The ink had run making them illegible, and impossible to cash in.

At first, I panicked, then I got angry. I was raging at my own stupidity but couldn't tell anyone what I had done. In those days, the final race was always televised. Geoff de Mulder, the trainer of the dog, had another dog in the race, called 'Sarah's Bunny.' As the race started, both dogs were way out in front. It was a nail- biting finale. Crazily, 'Desert Pilot' was beaten into third place, as 'Sarah's Bunny' raced home to victory. Insanely, I was devastated I had lost and yet, at the same time, elated that I hadn't won. I would have never been able to collect my winnings because of the ruined betting slips, which would have completely messed with my head.

A Night on the Tiles

I returned to the bank when I was offered a short-term contract to work in Bromley, Kent. Initially, they put me up in a hotel. On my first night there I had a couple of beers at the bar and then headed up to my room. Someone had told me that a good way to get creases out of your clothes was to hang them on the shower rail, turn the bathroom hot taps on and let the steam smooth out the creases. Taking their advice I switched on the taps, closed the bathroom door, and went to bed.

On waking next morning, I could hardly believe my eyes; almost all the tiles had fallen off the bathroom wall. I was freaking out, wondering how

I was going to explain what had happened. Being young and not very savvy, I thought I would have to pay for the damage. In those days I didn't have a credit card or any type of security. I made my way to reception to face the music. When I told the receptionist what had happened, she was equally shocked and started to apologise. Apparently, the bathroom had only been re-tiled the day I arrived and I should have never been put in that room. Relieved that it wasn't my fault, I set off to the bank to start my first day in my new job.

Work in Europe

It wasn't long before I was asked to go back to Belgium to work in Antwerp for five months. Once there, I didn't gamble during the week, but I was writing cheques for myself and stockpiling money. It meant I could have a good gambling session when I got home.

Returning to Belgium was fantastic. The people in the office were so friendly and most of them spoke perfect English. A typical day would start early. At lunchtime we would all eat out together and once work was finished, we would meet up again later and go out for a meal and drinks, not returning to the hotel until the early hours. The money was good, and I was able to claim expenses for meals and hotel bills.

The bank also paid for flights home at the weekend. Despite having a wife and two kids back home, I was living the life of a single man. Once home, my salary would go into my account, and the cheques I had written would be cleared. This left plenty of spare cash to use in the bookies. It was a difficult balancing act. Sadly, my time in Belgium came to an end. It was time to go back to Salford and face reality.

Not long after my return home I was relocated to Orpington in Kent. I went down first my wife came to join me six months later. We moved into a new-build house on a small housing estate. Our third child, a beautiful daughter, was born a year later. Thankfully, this time the pregnancy went to full term. I had been so worried after the premature birth of our second little boy and was relieved that our daughter was delivered safely. We brought her home to our little house and settled down to our daily routine.

Working in Bromley was great; like Antwerp, it was busy and vibrant. I soon joined the Coventry City London Supporters Group. Working through the week, I travelled to the football at weekends. I also joined the supporters club football team that played regularly at Wormwood Scrubs. In my favourite position as goalkeeper, I was enjoying being part of a team again.

My wife didn't settle so easily. Understandably, she missed her family. With three young children to care for, she must have been very lonely at times. I was so wrapped up in my own activities that I didn't really think about the impact it was having on her, living so far away from friends and family. She knew that I was gambling again, but not the true extent of it. I was getting better at covering my tracks.

I was asked to go to work in Madrid helping their documentary services department for a short period. The Mediterranean climate suited me. The office wasn't quite as friendly as Antwerp, but the bank was situated in the centre of Madrid, surrounded by tapas bars and shops. I spent much of my free time eating out and soaking up the atmosphere. On my return to England my wife said she wanted to go back to Salford. Life with me was becoming more and more unpredictable and I was often absent. I could understand why she wanted to leave, but I was reluctant to give up my new lifestyle. We decided to think about it.

On a red-hot day that summer I was on a winning streak, gambling all through my lunch hour. I decided to try my luck and pay my first, and as it turned out, my last, visit to Catford dogs' racetrack.

That evening, one of the bookies from Orpington High Street had a pitch on the rail. He was a familiar face in unfamiliar surroundings. I stuck out like a sore thumb that night, dressed as I was in white jeans and a white sweatshirt, with a blue flash across the front. I thought I looked 'the business.'

Well, it was the late 1980s. I continued my winning streak throughout the evening my ego was well boosted. Around 10.00 p.m. I decided to head for home.

My winnings were stuffed in my pockets, down my socks, in my shoes and yes, even down my underpants. As I walked out of the stadium, I got the feeling I was being followed. The faster I walked, the faster the footsteps came behind me. Glancing over my shoulder I saw two men. One of them was holding a knife, which flashed in the streetlights. They were about ten yards behind me. Sprinting off towards the High Street, a black cab stopped when the driver saw me frantically flagging him down. Once in the cab I screamed at him to

"Get me out of here!"

I never went back to that racetrack.

On the back of my winnings, I bought myself a suit for every day of the week. I could at least look the part, even if I was covering up a very different reality. Eventually, when I began losing heavily again, I returned the suits to the store to get my money back, to cover my losses. The roller coaster of my life rumbled on, as the gambling spiralled out of control.
I just loved the buzz and the culture, the way that you could lose yourself in the City. There were so many places and opportunities to gamble. I did try casinos, but it was the dogs, horses and football I loved most. Inevitably, things came to a head.

Mumps

In the January of 1987 I started to feel ill during a Coventry v Tottenham match at Highfield Road. My ears and neck really hurt. Sweat was pouring out of me and I felt weak and faint. Walking out after the match, I fell down the stairs. Everyone just stepped over me as I lay sprawled out and helpless. They probably all thought I was drunk. My mate, Colin, picked me up and drove me home. The following Monday, feeling seriously ill, I finally made it to the G.P. surgery. I had a raging temperature, my ears stuck out like Dumbo the elephant, and my testicles were absolutely huge. The doctor took one look at me and said,

"Mumps."

My wife was worried that our boys might catch mumps from me, so she packed her bags and took the kids back home to Salford. Eventually I got better and returned to work but my wife never came back to live in Kent.

On my own I got on with going to work, watching and playing football and gambling like mad.

The following May the 1987 Cup Final was looming and amazingly Coventry were going to play Spurs. Months earlier I had already placed a large bet on my team to win the F. A. Cup Final. After the quarter final someone offered me one hundred pounds cash for my betting slip. Being a gambler it seemed like a good deal. The chances of us winning was still unimaginable to me. I was desperate for money to feed my addiction so I gladly took the cash. The day of the Cup Final soon came around. The day finally dawned. It was a gloriously sunny day. I met my friend Colin at Orpington train station. We travelled up to the City of London to meet everyone for a pre-match drink. Later we travelled to Wembley where I was to meet my brother who was travelling down from Coventry.

I arrived at one o clock expecting my brother to be there. Unfortunately there was a problem on the railway so his train didn't arrive until two thirty; by which time I was getting stressed wondering where he was, He had my ticket and I just wanted to get into the stadium.

The atmosphere inside the ground was off the scale. The match that followed was regarded as one of the greatest Cup Finals of all time. Coventry against all the odds won the match 3 – 2 in extra time. The match winner supplied by Spurs captain Gary Mabbutt who scored an own goal by a deflection off his knee. The crowd was going wild. I travelled back to Coventry to stay at my parent's house overnight so I could see the team parade the cup through the streets of Coventry. Everywhere was decked in sky blue. Over three hundred thousand people lined the streets to welcome the team home.

On the Sunday evening I travelled back to Kent. After the euphoria of the weekend I finally came down to earth realising I had sold my betting slip two months earlier for a paltry hundred quid I would have won thousands, instead I was in despair and angry at my stupidity. Including my lack of faith in my team! It was shortly after that my depression and anxiety kicked in. I went AWOL from work.

I was too ill to shop or do anything. The man next door was dying of cancer. I could hear him coughing all day and all night. It was a desperate few weeks. Running out of food, I was becoming seriously hungry and depressed. The gas had been cut off, and I was surviving on dried pasta, cereal and tap water. The phone had been cut off too, so I couldn't call anyone. I kept the curtains closed day and night, refusing to answer the door, or open the growing pile of mail that arrived each day. I was completely housebound, unshaven and unkempt.

One day, I did open the door. A man and a woman from the bank stood on the doorstep. The look on both of their faces was enough to tell me that I looked as horrendous as I felt. Grey, gaunt and unshaven, I had dropped several stones in weight and my clothes hung on my emaciated frame. I wearily let them into the house. Pouring out my story. I could see that they were horrified.

They had no idea I was a compulsive gambler. To be honest, I don't know why I gave them all that information. I was obviously, physically and mentally ill. I could have got a sick note from my doctor, but I was too exhausted and defeated to bother.

Pouring out my whole sorry tale, about my addiction and the problems I was having, I told them I had attended Gambler's Anonymous at Westminster. I didn't tell them that I thought I was so much better than the people I had seen huddled on the benches at the meetings. Still in shock, they told me to clean myself up and come to work the next day. They obviously cared about my situation. All that they said gave me some hope that everything would be fine. Their understanding gave me the push I needed to get my act together.

The next day, arriving at the bank bright and early, I headed towards the lift. I was so glad to be back, with the nightmare of the past few weeks behind me. It was another fresh start. Full of anticipation at being given a second chance, I had good intentions to settle down to a new way of life, I never wanted to end up that low and isolated again. Walking to the lift, my way was blocked by security men. They ushered me to the information desk where they handed me a plastic bag containing the contents of my desk. They told me that my services were no longer required. Stunned and embarrassed, I didn't know what to say or do. Fighting to stay calm, I didn't even protest. I asked to see my manager but was refused. I should have probably asked to see a union rep, but dazed and confused as I was, I didn't have the words, or the energy to argue. Picking up my belongings, I walked out of the door and headed straight into the nearest bookies. My wife refused to come back from Salford. I had no choice but to put the house on the market. It sold quickly, making a healthy profit. Sad to be leaving, I packed up my few belongings and went to Coventry. Once my wife knew I had sold the house and had left Orpington she said that we could get back together despite reservations from her family.

Now that I was unemployed, I was earnestly looking for any work that would pay the bills and put food on the table. Over the next few years two more babies followed in quick succession: two beautiful boys, making it four boys and a girl. Initially we had a small terraced house which only had two bedrooms so we managed to get a council house near to my wife's parents. The problem was it only had three bedrooms. It obviously wasn't big enough for a family of seven. Reluctantly, we allowed our daughter to go to live with her grandparents. It was only across the road from us and was only ever meant to be an interim arrangement until we could get a bigger house. Unfortunately, the bigger house never materialised, so she lived long-term with her grandparents and came over to join us for meals or to be with her brothers. Other than this, she mostly stayed away. Eventually, things just stayed as they were, and any influence I might have had on her life, for good or bad, was taken away. As ever, things were happening that made me feel out of control, but I had to accept that I was a big part of the problem. My wife's parents weren't very forgiving and made it quite clear how they felt about my behaviour. The 'blue-eyed boy' who had come to live with them years before had been replaced by an addict, who couldn't do anything right. I knew I was probably an embarrassment and a disappointment to them.

Unbelievably, after all that had happened, I continued to gamble at every opportunity. On numerous occasions I went with a mate to Winsford dog track. He had a greyhound and we went there with the intention of winning. A greyhound has to have a series of trials before it can race. It helps the track owner to determine which grade the greyhound will race in, based on its average times over a certain distance. It was well known at the time that some owners would try to manipulate the outcome by feeding, drugging or over-exercising the animal before the trial. This would have the effect of slowing the dog down, by fractions of a second, on the day of the actual race. When the dog was primed for racing and totally fit, the times for that dog would improve, giving it a better chance of winning. On those occasions, massive bets would be placed in anticipation of a win. It was a cruel practice, but sadly a common one.

I can remember one evening, after a number of trials, the dog was registered to run. I was asked to walk the dog around the track to show it off before the race, and to place it in the traps.

My mate was busy lumping on huge bets for the both of us. I was buzzing. The atmosphere was electric, with the noise from the bookies on the pegs and the punters raucous conversation and laughter, and the sound of the

PA system calling out the names for the next race. The lights were really bright and there was a carnival atmosphere on the track. Despite all the glamour of the evening, I am sure there were some poor souls crumpled in despair somewhere, hungry and needing help, but I wasn't thinking of them. I was only thinking about the money we stood to win when our dog romped home victorious.

The track marshal asked us to place the greyhounds in the traps. As I did, I accidentally stood on our dog's paw. As my size eleven feet and fourteen stones of weight landed on that poor dog's paw, it let out a loud yelp of pain. There was no time to check for damage; I just bundled the injured animal into the trap and hoped for the best. The bell rang, and the electronic hare set off around the edge of the track. Seconds later the traps flew open and all the dogs set off in pursuit. I was relieved to see that our dog had got off to a good start.

The race was known as a 'middle-distance stayers' race. Our dog was known to race 'off the pace' but had an ability to then finish fast. As we watched, everything seemed to be going to plan. Our dog was flying towards the finish and we were screaming it home, but it lost by a short head in a photo finish. We stared at the results board in shock. We both lost a considerable amount of money that night. Later, as he was washing the dog's paws to remove the sand from the track, my mate noticed that its paw was bruised and swollen. I never told him what happened then, or since. If you ever get to read this mate, I'm sorry. Thankfully, the dog was fine and went on to win many other races. We hatched a similar plan at Bolton and more than made our money back.

Happy days!

CHAPTER TWO

Sent to Coventry

It was a blazing hot Saturday afternoon. Mum and Dad were sitting in the back garden at our home in Coventry. The garden was my dad's pride and joy. The flower beds were well stocked with dahlias, roses, and numerous varieties of shrubs. Sweet peas grew up the outside wall of the garage, and apple and pear trees framed the garden at the far end. The most striking feature of the garden was the perfect lawn, which looked like a bowling green. Cutting the grass was the only thing that Dad ever allowed me to do. I was as much a perfectionist as he was.

I was staying at my parents' home, having literally been sent to Coventry as a result of a confession I had made to my wife. It was the final straw for her. It came after a gambling spree in Southport, I had gone home and told my wife about it. Predictably, what followed was a massive row. Having effectively turned her life upside down and inside out, I grabbed my keys and walked out of the house. I drove off, not knowing where I was going. I drove around Salford aimlessly and slept in the car for the best part of a week. Eventually, some friends took me in and let me have a shower and get cleaned up. They must have told my father-in-law where I was because he turned up and practically frog-marched me home. He was so angry, there was no point trying to reason with him. I was allowed to go into the house to get a bag of clothes and essentials. I was literally in the house for a few minutes. My brother-in-law sat in the driver's seat of his car, ready to drive me to my parents' home in Coventry. I was told to "**** off" and not come back. Issuing threats all over the place I knew this was it, my time had run out. There was no returning from this. I was sent to Coventry, which is how I came to be standing in my parents' garden.

Dad spoke.

> "You're going to have to go back up north. Your mother is far too ill, and we can't have you upsetting your brother before his big day."

My brother's "big day" was a bowling final. I didn't know it then, but Mum's cancer had returned. She had been diagnosed with breast cancer some years earlier. I could see that she really wanted to take care of me, but couldn't cope with this wreck of a son who had literally been dumped on her doorstep. Besides, I don't think either of them could cope with the thought of leaving me alone in the house. For all they knew, I might have sold off the family silver before they returned.

The Shop

My wife and I had managed a greengrocer's, off-licence and sandwich shop, in Salford, for some years before we separated. The people who previously owned it had won a large amount of money, and agreed to let us run the shop on a rental basis. I had been gambling heavily for a while, and as a result, had put the business into financial difficulty.

It was a cash rich business. We worked there together, putting in long hours from early in the morning until late at night, until we separated for the second time and were divorced. It wasn't always an easy place to work. There were a number of attempted break-ins and threats. We had to be on our guard against thieves and potentially violent intruders, who were looking for cigarettes, cash and booze to steal. That being said, the biggest threat to the stability of the business was me. I couldn't keep my hands out of the till. The draw of the cash was too much of a temptation for a compulsive gambler like me. I used to gamble further and further afield to make sure that nobody knew me in order to hide what I was doing from my wife and family. I reasoned that if I won 'big' we could take the business to the next level.

Then it happened. I actually did win big, at Cheltenham one week. I won over £90,000! With that amount of money I could have easily paid off the debts, bought a van for the business, taken us all on holiday AND still had change. Sadly, I put every penny of that money back into gambling, and blew an additional £30,000 of the business money in a few days. I was drawing out larger and larger sums of money from the business account to feed my addiction, and buying less stock, spacing it out on the shelves in an attempt to hide the fact that there was less and less produce for customers to buy.

My wife, having now come to realise the extent of the financial mess we were in, and sick and tired of the stress, the arguments and the instability of our lives, had had enough. I didn't blame her for feeling the way she did. The constant stress was exhausting for both of us. My greatest sadness, and regret, was that I didn't get a chance to say goodbye to my five kids. I loved them all so much, and it must have seemed that I had completely abandoned them. They were still young at that time, and the youngest really didn't understand why I had left them so abruptly. Ending up back at my parent's home in Coventry, was the worst of all situations for me. I was sinking ever deeper into depression and felt completely hopeless. I had no idea what I was going to do next, or if there was even a way out of the mess I had created.

Bolton Salvation Army Hostel

A Salvation Army collection bag had been posted through the letterbox at my parents' house. It had a contact number, which Dad called. He found out they had a hostel in Bolton, with room to take me in. Ever efficient, he bought me a one-way ticket to Bolton, and that same day drove me to

Coventry train station. I just did as I was told. I couldn't argue with him; I was a complete emotional wreck. It was the day of a total solar eclipse. As the train pulled into Manchester, all the office workers stood outside, or at their windows, looking upwards through special glasses. It was growing darker and eerily silent. I stepped off the train into a twilight city. To me, it seemed like an omen. Things were about to get much worse. Boarding the connecting train to Bolton, I fought to keep my emotions in check. I kept my head down to avoid eye contact with other passengers, hoping that no one would recognise me. I needn't have worried; everyone in the carriage was craning their necks to see what was happening in the sky.

The Bolton branch of the Salvation Army was on the edge of Bolton town centre. It took me ages to find it. Like most men, I didn't like to ask for directions very often. I knocked on the door, terrified of what was on the other side. A pleasant enough bloke invited me in. He led me to a room to be 'processed.' There were lots of forms to fill in for benefits, and personal details to be logged.

He asked if there were any relatives they should contact. Hardly! I had been sent from Salford to Coventry by one set of family and dumped on a one-way train to Bolton by the other. All alone, without family or friends, I answered all his questions. Later that day I had yet another interview, with one of the other officers, to talk through the reasons why I had ended up there. He listened patiently to my tale of woe. When the interview was over, he told me I would have to go to the Jobcentre

The Jobcentre was a severe looking government building in Bolton centre. Waiting to be seen, I crossed my legs; looking down I noticed, for the first time, that my shoes were split and I had holes in the soles. It turned out I wasn't entitled to any benefits, because, according to them, I already had a share in a business. The problem was, I was unable to remember any details about it, which just made everything more difficult. As far as I knew, my now ex-wife was still running the greengrocer business. Since I had not heard anything from her, I couldn't tell them what the state of play was. I was given an emergency loan to buy some shoes and some food. I promptly left the building and gambled most of it.

I needed work desperately as I didn't have any income. I decided to go back to a place I had worked before to see if they had any positions I always got on well there, I was sure if I could just speak to my old manager, I would be offered some work. I didn't care what it was. Walking into the reception area. I went up to the desk and asked to see the manager. The look on the receptionist's face shocked me. She looked me up and down and then asked me to leave. Despite my best efforts to keep clean, the smell of the hostel clung to me – a heady mixture of disinfectant, old school dinners and musty damp clothes. I only had one change of clothes, and they were becoming threadbare. I didn't really look in mirrors, but now, looking in the glass door of the building, I saw what everyone else saw.

A scruffy, smelly vagrant.

At night I would lock myself in my room. It was tiny. Clean and sparse, it contained a single bed and a wardrobe. To me it seemed like a prison cell; the walls were painted beige and a minute window looked out onto a ring road. The window couldn't be opened very wide in case you tried to jump out. My room smelled strongly of disinfectant as it was close to the toilet and shower block. Every morning I woke up really early, so that I would be the first one to have a shower. I tried to keep clean, and despite the lack of clothes and possessions, I still thought I was a cut above anyone else in there. I didn't like to eat there, I survived by drinking gallons of water. I could get the odd sandwich or 'end of the day' cheap stuff from the supermarkets. Pounding the streets all day, I lost even more weight.

The worst thing of all was the loneliness. Without any friends or family, I retreated inside myself. One guy who had been in the hostel a few weeks longer than me, told me that someone had hung themselves in my room a few weeks earlier. The thought of that desperate man haunted me at night; there were so many occasions when I wanted to do the same. It scared me to think about what I might do.

You had to leave the hostel during the day; it was a good thing the weather was warm. I would sit in front of the town hall on a bench or pass the time walking around the town. Old work colleagues or friends would sometimes bump into me. Some saw me and turned away, only a few stopped to talk. Desperate to gamble but almost penniless, I refused to beg. I remember one lady I knew took pity on me; she took me home and made me something to eat, and then took me back to Bolton. A random act of kindness, for which I was very grateful.

Returning to the 'Sally Army' hostel each evening was intimidating. At night the building sounded hollow and noisy. Every time someone closed a door, it clanged shut. Shouting and confrontation was the norm. The only security was a guard, who sat in reception all night. I got talking to someone who was using the hostel as a bail address, he had just done a long stretch in jail for burglary. Addicted to cocaine, he would tell me tales about the things he had done in order to feed his habit.

One day I decided to wash my jeans. I only had two pairs. The pair I washed got robbed out of the washing machine. I couldn't believe it! Even the clothes on my back were being stolen from me. Aware that I couldn't continue this way indefinitely I started to look for jobs in earnest. A security firm was advertising and so I walked there for the interview. Amazingly, they offered me the job. I lasted three days. Mentally I was in bits, and I couldn't stop crying. I told them I couldn't handle it and went back to the hostel. Despite it being an alien place to me, it was the only place of safety, but the longer I was in there the more suicidal I became. In a desperate state, I wanted to make everything all right, to make it up to my family, somehow. I missed my kids desperately. Full of remorse, anger and frustration, I couldn't see a way out of the mess I was in. I spent the majority of my day alone, speaking to no one. I really had nowhere to go and nothing to do.

It was then the 'voices' started;

"Go on, kill yourself, it's the only way out."

"You're worthless; no one will miss you. Even your own family can't stand you near them."

"Everyone will be glad that you're dead. It will be a relief."

I didn't know what the voices were or where they came from, but fighting them off, and dealing with the constant urge to kill myself, was exhausting and terrifying. I fought to stay in control from the incessant chatter in my ear. At times, I found I was talking back to myself in an attempt to make it stop. I would think about all the ways I could kill myself. What would be the best way? It both scared and comforted me to think I could stop everything at any time I chose. Normality was slipping away from me. I couldn't even get any respite at night, because I couldn't sleep in the tiny room full of my own thoughts, like inner voices, and the threat of menace.

After years of gambling, lying, abusing and thieving, I was angry at everyone and everything. I felt a terrible failure as a son, a husband, and father to my five children. I was beaten, broken and desperate, despised by everyone who knew me - including myself.

Over the next three days I stockpiled paracetamol, buying small amounts from different shops. Then one afternoon, using my last few pounds, I bought a bottle of whisky. Leaving the hostel in the early hours, I walked through the town centre towards the bus station. Opening the whisky, I started to drink and swallow the pills. After taking all of the tablets and draining the whisky bottle, I sat down and started to drift away. The concrete floor was hard and cold; I couldn't move and started to drift off to sleep. I could hear people calling to me but they sounded so far away. The sound of voices grew fainter, drowned out by the high-pitched scream of sirens. I was taken to Bolton General Hospital where they pumped my stomach - an awful, violent experience. Then they gave me charcoal to eat. I protested because it tasted disgusting, but above all, I was furious I was still alive.

The next thing I remember was waking in a hospital side ward, with my eldest son sitting at my bedside. Someone from the hospital must have got in touch with my family to let them know what had happened to me. I had a drip in my right arm and continued to drift in and out of consciousness. Someone was talking to my son.

"We think we got most of what he had taken, out of him."

I was discharged the following morning without any mental health assessment. As I walked away from the hospital, my ex-father-in-law appeared and picked me up in his car. I don't remember how, or even why, he was there; he dropped me at the car park near Bolton town centre. As I was getting out of the car he turned on me, telling me not to try that again. My relationship with him had always been difficult. Now was no different.

One afternoon I had walked from Bolton to Four Lane Ends at Walkden, to see one of my sons on his birthday. His grandad was with him. My son looked so small in his cricket whites, holding his new cricket bat. He was really timid but seemed happy to see me. I was told to pull myself together, and that if I cried, I would never see him again. His grandad sat in the car while I spoke to my son, who told me he had been picked to play for Salford the following Sunday.

On the Sunday in question I walked to Atherton to watch him play. I sat at the back so he wouldn't see me or get upset during the match. I did manage to speak a few words with him at the end of the afternoon. I missed him with all my heart. It was a physical, indescribable pain that didn't go away. I grieved for my kids. To me, it was as though I had suffered five bereavements. I knew that they would be suffering too. Despite all I had done, I really loved them. I had spent lots of time with them, especially the boys playing football and cricket. I coached teams they played in, and in the summer, we would be out on the cricket ground and the golf course, often until it grew dark. I missed being with them and couldn't understand why I wasn't being allowed to see them. I was scared they would forget all about me, or that they would hate me, and wouldn't understand I was trying really hard to get to see them.

CHAPTER THREE

Homeless

Homeless. In the past, whenever I heard that word it always made me think of drunks, drug addicts, down and outs, and tramps. I reckoned it was a shameful state they had brought on themselves.

Not many people had much sympathy for those who were homeless in the past. Thankfully, today, we see homelessness differently, and there is more support available for people who find themselves in that situation. People end up homeless for a variety of reasons, one of the most common being a breakdown in family relationships. Addiction to gambling was the root cause of my problems, but a breakdown in family relationships was the thing that pushed me out onto the pavements of Bolton.

I was homeless in the fullest sense of the word. Leaving the Salvation Army hostel seemed like a good idea at the time. Somehow, I still felt I could make it on my own and didn't need anyone's help. I wasn't thinking logically, or clearly, but staying in the hostel felt like a scary place to be. Although the officers were great and tried to be really helpful to all the residents, the hostel housed a mixed bag of humanity, and staying there was making me more and more fearful. But as I was about to find out, making yourself voluntarily homeless is one of the worst things you can do if you want help from the state. Having "no fixed abode," means you couldn't register for benefits, or access help from social services. The situation is not that much better today, especially for young, single men.

I spent my days drifting around Bolton, and Manchester city centre. I would walk for miles, and then sit on benches near the shopping centre or in the parks. The early evenings and night times were the worst. The town centre would empty around 5.00 p.m. leaving the streets as vast and lonely places.

As night fell, more people would come into town, congregating around the clubs and pubs. That meant more chances of threatening behaviour. I tended to leave the town centre in the evening.

I used to sleep outside a hotel, near the air vents in the basement where it was warmer.
Sometimes, one of the porters would take pity on me and allow me in to get cleaned up and have a warm drink. The temperature in the early hours of the morning would drop dramatically. Sleeping out without a sleeping bag or blankets, was desperately cold and damp.

Occasionally, I met people I knew, who would feed me or give me a bed for the night. As time went on, my mental state grew worse. I was completely paranoid, still hearing the voices in my head, and deeply depressed. I wasn't feeling a bit down or low in mood, or unhappy. No. This was a deep, black, deadening feeling. I was almost emotionless, with a constant feeling of foreboding and unease hanging over me.

The next attempt to take my own life was treated much more seriously by the professionals.

I had nothing more to lose. Without friends or family, I spent my days and nights alone, with little conversation or interaction with any human beings. This time I swallowed a cocktail of different tablets; whatever I could get my hands on. Unravelling mentally, I could see only death as the way out of the constant pain and turmoil I was in. After all, I would be doing everyone a favour. It wouldn't be an act of selfishness to stop living. I would be one less problem to deal with. I wasn't sent back to the streets after this attempt, this time it was for real. I was assessed by the mental health team and admitted to Cheadle Royal Hospital.

On Being a Patient

Cheadle Royal then was an old, Victorian, brick building on the outskirts of Manchester. I was terrified by the thought of being admitted to a psychiatric hospital. Strangely though despite my fears, when I was told I was being admitted for observation and for my own safety, I didn't resist. The ward became my home for the next few weeks. A psychiatrist visited me and prescribed some medication.

I spent the whole time crying.

Initially, I was in a room on my own, feeling terrified. People were coming and going all day and night. It was an old ward, with a long ward off the main corridor. Eventually, I was moved out onto the main ward. At night I could hear people shouting and crying. Alarm bells went off well into the night. The ward was dimly lit and you could hear everything. I couldn't believe what was happening to me. There were huge windows along both walls, through which you could watch the planes landing at Manchester Airport. They flew so low over the hospital it felt like you could reach up and touch them. I envied the people on those planes, who could go where they wanted, when they wanted.

From Cheadle Royal, I was transferred to Meadowbrook Hospital in Salford. Exhausted and apprehensive, I wasn't sectioned but advised to be admitted voluntarily for treatment.

Meadowbrook was a modern unit. Each ward had individual rooms, which I thought was even more frightening than the open wards in Cheadle Royal. It was very busy, but above all it was noisy. Security alarms were constantly blaring – they emitted a piercing sound like an ambulance siren. You could hear the staff running in the direction of the sound, although you couldn't see anything.

The wards were mixed, with both male and female patients, and built around a central courtyard with a garden. There was a shared dining room and a television room. I didn't know the system, so I didn't know who all the staff members were. There were nurses, doctors and security guards in constant attendance.

During the day it was tolerable, but at night the ward took on a menacing air. Patients would start kicking off at all hours; my nerves were constantly on edge. I had arrived on the ward in the middle of the day and was interviewed by one of the staff nurses. He asked about my mood, my background, and what had brought me there. He asked about my next of kin, and I gave the names of my ex-wife and my eldest son. It soon became apparent that my ex-wife didn't want to be contacted. I sat alone, not knowing what was going to happen next or how long I was going to be in hospital. The uncertainty made me agitated. Despite feeling so lonely, I didn't want to talk to anyone. I just wanted to wipe out the past few months and start over. That wasn't about to happen anytime soon.

Monday was ward round day. If you were well enough, you were taken to a room full of nurses and doctors (including the consultant) to discuss your progress. To my tortured mind, it felt like being called up in front of a judge and jury. These people had the power to keep you inside or set you free.

In the evenings, most people left their rooms and went to the TV room. If it was quiet, one of the nurses would sit and chat with us. It was there that I got to know some of my fellow 'inmates.'

There was a young man, who, I found out, was in a similar situation to mine. He was also suffering from depression, but even so, he had a brilliant smile and we often spent time talking together. An older woman who had suffered from a stroke was with us too. The young man did get visitors but we, never had any.

A month after my admission, my young friend was allowed to go home for weekends. He would be very agitated when he came back, and his mum was really worried about him.   I don't know the details of what really happened, but hours after the last time he was discharged, he hung himself in a wood near the hospital. A member of the nursing staff came to tell me what had happened. I guess they didn't want me to find out through the news or ward gossip; I was devastated. He had become my closest, and only, friend. The staff put me on suicide watch for some time after. A week after his death, the staff asked if I wanted to attend the funeral. I said I really wanted to pay my respects. On the day two nurses escorted me to the church, which just happened to be around the corner from my old home.

The church was packed with his friends and family. It was difficult for me to attend and I left the church feeling desperately sad. For some time after the funeral, the staff kept asking me how I felt about his suicide and if I had similar thoughts and feelings. I had to admit to having suicidal thoughts. There was nothing positive for me to look forward to. How was I ever going to find my way back into the real world or live a normal life?

One day I sneaked off the ward and walked to my home. I knew my ex-wife would be in the local cricket club that night. There was a big stand-off. I was shown the door by some of her friends. I was outside, sitting on a bench, when my eldest son turned up. He took me back to the unit. I had only wanted to speak to her to try to sort things out. She must have been scared when I turned up. I arrived back on the ward really agitated. My son was so worried about me. He was just eighteen, and had been left shouldering the responsibilities which should have been mine. He became my only link with the other kids.

I tried all sorts of avenues in an attempt to get my ex-wife to speak to me. One day I rang the business; it was the umpteenth time I had rung. On this occasion her friend answered. She wouldn't allow me to speak to her, which just made me angrier. I threatened that if she didn't bring my wife to the phone, I would 'fry her alive' when she was asleep. I knew the minute I said it, it was a terrible thing to say! Less than half an hour later, two police officers arrived on the ward looking for me. I was escorted to the interview room. They told me they had received a complaint and asked how serious my threats were. They understood that I was ill but they wanted to know if I meant what I had said. I burst into tears, full of remorse. I was given a verbal warning. They explained to me that despite the fact I was an in-patient in a psychiatric ward, this did not mean that it was ok for me to go around making threats on people's lives. I promised I wouldn't do anything like that again and there the matter rested.

My depression continued, and the voices in my mind were incessant. One day, a young lad turned up on the ward in a really dishevelled state. He didn't have any spare clothes. I can remember giving him one of my two shirts. I didn't really get to know him as he was moved on pretty quickly. I felt good about giving him the shirt; it proved I still had a small spark of humanity and compassion left in me.

Security were regularly called for, during my time there. One night they arrived on the ward in large numbers to engage with a patient who had barricaded himself in his room. I could hear them shouting and the patient screaming back at them. The atmosphere was intense and the noise unsettling. I stayed in my room, frightened about what would happen next.

I got to know one of the male nurses quite well. He had a broken marriage himself, and he kept telling me that he knew how I must be feeling. There didn't seem to be a lot of understanding of gambling addiction at that time. He encouraged me to attend Gamblers Anonymous meetings in Bolton. I was feeling anxious and distressed at that time. In order to be able to attend Gamblers Anonymous, I would first need to overcome my increasing feeling of agoraphobia.

Initially, to help me overcome these feelings, the nurses would take me to the dining room in the main hospital for a coffee. Then they would walk me back to the ward. Gradually, I was taken out of the building and helped to get onto a bus and eventually someone would meet me further along the route. The journeys got slightly longer each time I went out. My anxiety started to lessen and my fear of being outdoors diminished. I dawned on me that I didn't know how to function in the real world. The hospital had become my safe place and I was reluctant to leave it. I had nowhere else to go and nobody would be waiting to meet me.

It was as though I had been locked away and not given another thought. I knew I must have behaved so terribly in the eyes of those who knew me, for no one to even enquire if I was dead or alive. I had rung my Mum on her birthday. Dad answered. When I told him where I was, he said he expected I might have ended up somewhere like that. He never enquired about me again the whole time I was in hospital. I never did get to speak to my Mum. I missed her so much, but she always did what my Dad said. From the day I left home at seventeen, my relationship with my parents had been strained. When I was married, they only ever visited occasionally, and then not for very long. They rarely saw the kids, and really treated my ex-wife badly.

As I settled into the hospital routine, I got to know other people. I met some who were experts at playing the system. It was my first real encounter with drug addicts. Interestingly, they behaved very much like I did when I was in action as a gambler. It was fascinating, and frightening at the same time, due to the unpredictability of their behaviour. It gave me some insight into how people must have felt around me, when I was being frightening and unpredictable, and craving for a bet.

As the months wore on, I started to go out into the garden, which unfortunately caused more problems. One girl became very fond of me. She would sit on my knee, stroking my face and my hair. I couldn't get rid of her. At any other time I might have been flattered, but I remained resistant to her demonstrations of affection. This went on for some time, with the 'bipolar beauty,' until one day a nurse came out and told her to leave me alone. She said she was only trying to cheer me up.

I saw lots of people I knew, either through business or family connections, that were visiting at the hospital. Sometimes I got to speak to them and would ask if they could get a message to my children. I don't know if they ever did pass on the messages. Patients came and went. Some got better or were moved onto other wards. Some went home, only to relapse and arrive back on the ward. It was like watching a revolving door. I, on the other hand, stayed exactly where I was. I must have been very sick, or maybe the fact I had nowhere to go to, was the thing that kept me there.

The whole build-up to Christmas and the Millennium was a very sad time for me. Patients who were well enough, were allowed home. I was left behind with a handful of other patients. As Christmas drew near, my mood dipped. I didn't receive one, single Christmas card, or a visit from anyone. It was as though I had been buried alive and left to rot. Was I such a terrible human being that no one could spare me a thought; even at Christmas? Even murderers in prison would have someone who cared about them. This felt worse than being in prison.

The staff did their very best to make it a happy time. The ward was decorated with trees and tinsel. We had lovely buffets and treats; someone sneaked a bottle of lager into my room to celebrate with on New Year's Eve. As the week wore on, I became more and more apprehensive. I imagined my family together, and my parents with my brother. I envisaged that everyone was glad I wasn't there. Not one of them would miss me; it made me feel sick, right to my very soul. Somehow, I made it through Christmas without incident, but New Year's Eve was looming, and my feelings of worthlessness were at an all-time low.

CHAPTER FOUR

~~God, Gasoline,~~

~~Gamblers'~~

Anonymous

It was cold and damp beneath the canopy of trees. I could see the main road from my bench on the edge of the park. Not one solitary soul had passed by. The roads were empty. I was cold, alone and surrounded by darkness. I began to wonder if anyone had raised the alarm yet. I had left the ward after breakfast; it was now ten o'clock at night. I had been walking for miles all over Salford, visiting places that held memories, not all of them good. Walking off the ward early that morning had been easy. Everyone was caught up with the Millennium celebrations of the night before. No one noticed as I slipped out of the main door to the ward and down the stairs into the street. Some police officers had passed by earlier, but no one had stopped to question me.

Walking through Buile Hill Park was painful. It brought back memories of my wedding day.

Our photographs had been taken in the park after our wedding at Salford Cathedral. Over the past few months I had spent a lot of time revisiting the park. That night it was a threatening, fearful place.

It was a hangout for addicts, drug dealers and the homeless, looking for a spot to lay their head down for the night. That night, even the homeless had found a better place to be. I walked around in the dark, following every path to make sure that no one was about. Knowing that the park was empty and I was totally alone, made me all the more determined to do what I had decided to do. I didn't want to be on this planet any longer. My family and friends had all turned their backs on me; the kids had been kept from seeing me. To destroy myself, seemed like the only way to end the constant, mental pain.

My Third Attempt at Suicide

I set myself to the task at hand, my thoughts were totally chaotic. First, standing on a picnic table I tried to hang myself, but couldn't quite get my tie to hold around the branch of the tree. I left it hanging there a sky blue tie with white dots it hung forlornly from the branch a marker of sorts.

Frustrated, I sat on the picnic table and picked up the petrol can I had bought earlier that evening. I didn't want to think too much about what I was going to do. Releasing the cap, I emptied the contents all over myself until my clothes were completely soaked in petrol. Fishing the cigarette lighter out of my pocket, I started to flick it on and off. Small sparks leapt from it, followed by a steady flame.

I screamed out to God,

"God if you really are there, you've got to help me."

Sobbing and broken, the petrol fumes filled my nostrils and stung my eyes.

I don't know that I believed in God, even though I was calling out to Him. If He was there, He hadn't done very much for me lately. My life had been pretty desperate so far. That night, alone in the darkness, I called out to the one person I wasn't sure even existed – and if He did exist - He almost certainly didn't have time to pay attention to a loser like me. At that very moment, two police officers stepped out from the trees behind me. One of them shouted to me,

"Nick, don't do it."

They approached me warily, all the time coaxing me to hand over the petrol can and lighter. It was a man and a woman. I can still remember, the woman had blonde hair cut in a short bob. I couldn't believe my eyes or my ears. Were they angels? Where on earth had they come from? Whatever and whoever they were, God had seemingly heard my cries.

They took me to the police van, parked a short distance away, and removed my petrol-soaked clothes, then wrapped me in a large, warm blanket. I let them take care of me. I was partly relieved and frustrated at the same time. They drove me back to Meadowbrook and took me up to the ward.

Strangely, no-one on the ward, neither staff nor patients, asked me where I had been all day. I was taken to the shower to wash off any remaining petrol, and then escorted to my room and given a sedative to help me sleep. I would love to have found out who those officers were that night so that I could thank them, but no one referred to them and I never saw them again.

One of the male nurses befriended me on my return to the ward. He talked to me about my marriage and my family. He told me something about his situation, which was very similar to mine, minus the addiction. He asked if I liked to play table tennis. I hadn't played for many years but agreed to give him a game. It turned out I still had the 'killer instinct.'. I hated losing and quickly stepped up. It was during this time I started to smile again. Thanks to him, and the regular exercise, my mood lifted and I began to feel better. As I improved, there was talk about discharging me. For the second time, I was put on a programme designed to give me the confidence to go outside. I was anxious about leaving the security of the ward, so the staff would get me to walk through the hospital to the nearest bus stop. I would get on the bus and go along a few stops. There would be someone waiting for me when I got off.

Paranoia

Not only did I have a fear of going outside, but I was also paranoid. I was constantly looking over my shoulder to see if anyone was following me. This was partly because I knew there were people out there who had loaned me money, which I hadn't repaid. There were also family members I dreaded bumping into. Despite these obstacles my confidence slowly grew, and I was able to take longer journeys and even go to the shopping centre. My life was starting to rebuild, from rock bottom.

A social worker was assigned to me. She interviewed me and asked where I might like to live if I was discharged. I can remember saying that I didn't want to live in a flat on my own. Someone mentioned the Richard Carr-Gomm Charity. It had been set up by Richard Carr-Gomm, an army officer, who, on returning home after World War Two, saw men and women who were left alone without family or a place to live. He was especially saddened to see ex-soldiers who were suffering from mental illness and shell shock. He decided to set up homes for them to live in which provided safe, sheltered housing. There were two homes in the area. One was near

Buille Hill Park, the other on Wellington Road, Eccles. I can remember the social worker saying that she thought the Wellington Road house would be the best one for me. So one afternoon I went to Eccles to see it.

It was a large, detached property with a mock Tudor front, and a garden, and was in the process of being refurbished. I would have a bedroom and an en-suite shower room, when it was completed. Initially, I would need to share the bathroom, as I did at the Sally Army. There was a huge kitchen, with fridges where you could store your food. Because I didn't smoke, I would be the only one to use the non-smoking TV room. I decided that this might be the place for me, so the staff secured a place and started to work with me, aiming at discharge into the community.

Wellington Road

I was finally discharged from hospital on Valentine's Day 2000. Not the best of days for me, but then, no day was going to be a good day. I walked from the hospital to Wellington Road, and by the time I reached there it was dusk. On my arrival, a support worker with long blonde hair, and wearing Doc Martins, interviewed me. I had a bag containing a couple of shirts and two pairs of trousers. There was a stack of forms to fill in for housing and other benefits. The forms freaked me out. I panicked, suddenly feeling out of my depth. I didn't understand all the questions or how to answer them. I kept them overnight, hoping that someone would help me to make sense of them the next morning.

I was happy to have a room to myself but didn't sleep well that first night. There were unfamiliar sounds and strangers' voices. I could hear noises out on the street, and a TV was on in the next room. The next day, I met a lovely support worker Lillian, she was gentle and quietly spoken, and seemed really caring. Sheila, the other support worker who ran the house, didn't suffer fools gladly and sounded quite stern, but underneath that tough exterior she had a heart of gold.

Eventually, the rooms were all upgraded. I got my own shower, and a small fridge to myself. It was better than storing food in the big fridges, in the kitchen. Often your food got stolen. There was a rota in the house to clean the communal areas but not everyone was very good at remembering when it was their turn.

I thought I was a lot more hygienic than the other lads, but I still had a lot to learn about humility. All in all, it was a good place to be. Wellington Road, and its various occupants, became home and family for the next eighteen months.

I was registered with a G.P., and a Community Psychiatric Nurse (C.P.N.) came to visit me. I was given about £45.00 a week, which had to pay for my food, clothes and transport. Consequently, I walked everywhere. In the first month I didn't venture too far. The hardest thing was trying to stay out of the bookies. There were nine other men in the house, who all had varying degrees of mental illness and addiction. For those like me, it was a place of safety, where we could rebuild our shattered lives. Lillian and Sheila, were really supportive and encouraging. We had regular chats to discuss how I was feeling and coping. Everyone had to do jobs in the house. Our rooms and all the communal areas had to be cleaned. Keeping my own room clean and tidy wasn't a problem, as I had hardly any possessions. I started working in the garden. I enjoyed gardening, it got me out of my room and into the fresh air.

In all my time there, I was never able to form really close friendships. There were people I spoke to, but I didn't let them get too close to me. I did start to attend Gamblers Anonymous (G.A.). There were meetings in Manchester, which I attended every week in an attempt to address my addiction. I found the meetings really helpful; there were lots of people there whose stories I could relate to.

Looking back over that whole year, it was a time of trying to recover and get some stability back into my life. To my delight, my eldest son visited me a few times in Eccles. I had a social worker whom I confided in. I told her that I really wanted to have some contact with my other children. She discouraged me at the time, saying she didn't think I was strong enough emotionally. With hindsight, this probably wasn't very good advice as it served to keep me apart from my kids. I couldn't even get to have supervised visits, and the longer I went without seeing them, the harder it got. I ended up being prescribed large doses of Prozac to keep my mood stable and prevent me from sinking back into depression. Gradually, I started to feel physically stronger, though still fragile emotionally.

I can't remember how it happened, or who arranged it, but that Easter I went into Manchester to meet up with two of my lads and my daughter. It had been arranged that I would meet them on my own. It was a disaster. I really should have met them with someone else present. I took them for something to eat. I just remember trying to treat them and make it special, but I couldn't stop crying.

The kids kept saying it was alright and were trying to comfort me. They were upset too. On the way home I had to get off the bus before them. Watching them go was terrible. I didn't know if, or when, I would see them again. As it happened, the kids were obviously upset by the whole thing, so their mum decided it was best to keep them from seeing me. I couldn't speak to her directly, and I didn't see them again until the following year, and then, only very briefly.

That October, Lillian suggested that a few of us should go on holiday somewhere. After much discussion we decided to go to Estartit, in Spain, for a week. I was looking forward to going somewhere different, where it would be warm. As it happened, it rained practically the whole time we were there. The highlight of the trip was going to Barcelona for the day.

I got to see the Nucamp Stadium. As an ardent football fan I thought it was fantastic. One of the lads wanted to have a leather belt made for him. We found a place, in a dark backstreet, where they made leather goods. Whilst it was being made, we went to a bar on the same street. It was full of locals who didn't speak any English. We must have made a strange couple; I was six feet two, and my mate 'T' was less than five feet two. We drew a lot of attention, but just kept smiling and ordering more beer.

It was really hot on the last day of our stay. I walked along the beach for miles. Finally, I was starting to realise there was a much better life out there for me than the life I had been living.

I returned from the trip feeling physically and mentally stronger. Lillian continued to encourage me to move on and stretch myself. For the first time, in a very long time, I began to see that there might be some hope of a future. I was looking at the jobs ads in the paper. One, which leapt out at me, was an advert for male escorts. There was a promise of earnings up to five hundred pounds a night. How hard could it be? I mean, how difficult can it be escorting women to dinner or the theatre. It could be quite pleasant, and I was looking ok. I scrubbed up quite well. I rang the number in the advert. Within two minutes of starting the conversation, it was obvious that I was well out of my depth. The lady on the end of the phone was lovely, as she explained exactly what the job entailed, and gently suggested that being an escort wasn't the best occupation and that I look elsewhere for work. I was so embarrassed. It hadn't crossed my mind what it might actually entail.

Thankfully, soon after, it was strongly suggested I apply for a volunteer job at the local Age Concern. At the interview I tried to sabotage my chances, by telling the woman interviewer I couldn't do the job and that I was unreliable. She refused to listen to my protests and told me I could start in the office, selling insurance, the following week. I loved it there. My self-confidence improved, and the work gave my days some structure and purpose. After a short time, they offered me some part-time paid hours. I was settling into the routine in the house, and slowly regaining confidence in myself and in my ability to work. I continued to attend G.A. meetings, and every day I succeeded in staying out of the bookies. It was a struggle, but I knew I had to get my life straightened out, especially if I was ever going to have any chance of seeing my kids again.

Despite living in a house with nine other men, I felt lonely. Whilst I knew it was a consequence of my addiction and behaviour, it was hard to think I might never see my family again.

PART TWO

DONNA

CHAPTER FIVE

Beginnings

My entry into this world was not an easy one. My mum was just nineteen years old, and my father, an Irishman, was somewhere working aboard a passenger liner on the high seas near Hong Kong, on the day I was born. Mum was seriously ill with eclampsia, and to save her life the obstetricians' induced labour. Several hours later I was dragged into the world by forceps, and being very premature and sick, I was immediately whisked off in an incubator to the Special Care Baby Unit. Mum was kept sedated in a darkened room to prevent her from having fits, and she didn't get to see me again for over two weeks. We were both fighting the first of many battles together, the battle for life itself. I was baptised in that incubator – a small scrap of humanity, not expected to survive. Against all the odds, I began to thrive and put on weight. We both went home some six weeks later.

My twin sisters were born nearly four years later, during Christmas 1961. I remember standing in the reception of the Maternity Unit in Oldham, wearing my brand-new Christmas present. It was a nurse's uniform, complete with hat, cuffs, fob watch and medical bag. I loved it. I proudly declared to the midwives on the ward that I would come back to work there when I was older. I did just that, qualifying as a midwife many years later. I worked there for six years. Looking through the nursery window at all the babies in their cots and asked if I could choose any that I wanted. I was gently told that it wasn't a shop and that the babies in the front two cots were my sisters. The neighbours were desperate for them to come home, as I had told them all that my mum had given birth to a black one and a white one. One of them was very fair, with red hair; her twin had dark hair. When the time came to go home, the precious nurse's uniform was packed away in the box with the smiley blonde staff nurse on the lid. We boarded the bus and as we got off the bus near home the precious Christmas present was left behind in the luggage compartment. Trying desperately to cope with his inconsolable four-year-old, Dad ran all the way to the bus station to see if it had been handed in. It hadn't. My little heart was broken. It was my first big lesson in life. The things you treasure can be taken from you in an instant, and there is nothing you can do about it.

The twins came home to live in our little terraced house in Oldham, with a shared yard and an outside loo. Ice formed on the inside of the windows in winter. We had a tin bath, which was filled each Friday night in front of the fire. Dad left the Navy to work on shore. My grandparents, whom I adored, lived two doors away. A few years later we all moved to a new housing estate. We were given a ground floor flat, with French windows which opened out onto our very own garden. It had three bedrooms, and a separate indoor loo and bathroom. We were in heaven.

We spent the first few weeks taking baths at every opportunity. No more Friday nights in the tin bath for us! The flat had central heating, so the house was always warm and cosy.

By the time I was eleven, Dad decided he was going back to sea. He joined the Merchant Navy. To me, he was an awesome figure, who would randomly appear at intervals wearing a naval uniform and peaked cap. He wasn't allowed to drink on board ship, so when the ship docked, him and his mates would hit the nearest bar. By the time he came home he would be quite merry. He could be hilariously funny, telling us about all the places he had been to, most of them not worth the bother, in his opinion. He would sing the old Irish songs in a flat monotone, whilst keeping time with the thud-thud-thud of his foot on the kitchen floor.

When sober, he was a quiet, shy man. But with a few whiskies inside him he could become loud and argumentative. That dad was a million miles from the dad who took me to the docks at Salford to see his ship and taught me how to row a boat on the local park's boating lake. I didn't understand addiction, or even whether to call it addiction. All I knew, was that this dad was different; that Mum was desperately unhappy and there were frequent rows. Looking back with greater insight, I can be more objective and understanding. Mum was amazing really. She cared for the three of us, mostly on her own, because Dad was away such a lot. She could do anything, decorate the house, re-wire plugs, and she worked full time. She took over the decorating after Dad had wallpapered the living room. He had hung the paper upside down and we spent many years trying not to look at the flowers which were blooming heads down with their stems in the air! I admired my Mum massively, but I don't think I ever told her that. My solution to getting into trouble was to stay outside for as long as possible, or to lose myself in books. I read anything I could get my hands on. The library was one of my favourite places. The other was church I loved going there. We went to the local Roman Catholic Church and school. We had nuns who taught at our school. Many people have horror stories about nuns, but all the sisters who taught me were very kind and caring women, who loved us. I wanted to be just like them when I grew up. So much so I think they thought they might have a little postulant on their hands. One of the sisters used to let me sit on her knee when I was little. I would hide under her huge veil and play with the big wooden beads that hung from her belt.

As I grew older, I was drawn to acting and dance; the more I could dress up and become someone else, the better. I also became more aware of boys. Coming from a house full of girls, boys held a fascination for me. I left school at sixteen and joined a nursing cadet scheme. Soon after, I met my future husband. He was three years older than me. We used to go to the same clubs. I was obviously underage, but that didn't deter me, or him. On turning eighteen I started nurse training, and we set a date to be married. All my friends were marrying young and it seemed like the logical, next step. We married one hot August day I was just twenty and couldn't wait to leave home. Dad was unimpressed. If I was going to be a nurse Dad wondered, why couldn't I join the Queen Alexandra's Nursing Corps and see something of the world. I didn't listen to him. I wish I had.

Instead, I ploughed on with our wedding plans. In the 1970s and even the early '80's, nursing was still pretty much seen as a vocation, and most married women were not accepted for training. The Matron was very much in charge of the hospital, which was like a mini township.

The night before the wedding I was sick with nerves, no longer sure that I wanted to get married. My beautiful dress and veil hung on the wardrobe door. I couldn't back out; everything was paid for, and people were coming from Ireland and Birmingham. Stuffing my fears into the far recesses of my mind, I told myself that everyone gets nervous the night before their wedding. Deep down, I knew what I knew. This marriage was not likely to last.

The marriage did, in fact, last for seven whole years. For six of them, my husband had been seeing other women. Somehow, during this time, I got through my general nurse training. The fact that I worked shifts, was perfect for him to cover his tracks. I went straight into midwifery training, which meant even more unsocial hours. To be fair to him, for a man used to having his mother do everything for him, I must have been a severe disappointment. I was not a domestic goddess, I could hardly boil an egg. The final straw came when he started an affair with a woman he worked with. The atmosphere at home was dreadful. Sick with anxiety, I stopped eating altogether. Finally, weighing just six and a half stones, and in the grip of anorexia nervosa, I looked and felt frail. I was being abused verbally and emotionally. I was repeatedly told to stop nagging, and that I was fat, ugly and useless. After a particularly upsetting phone call from his current woman, telling me everything he was getting up to, I finally snapped. I couldn't take any more stress. We were in serious debt. He had stopped paying the mortgage. Having tried so hard to keep my private life and work life separate for so long, my two worlds were on an unavoidable collision course.

I took a good look at myself one morning as I was getting dressed. For the first time, I could see myself as others saw me. The image in the mirror shocked me. I was literally skin and bone. My ribs and hip bones stuck out, my face gaunt with huge sunken eyes. The head of midwifery called me into her office soon after, and told me that if I didn't go to see my doctor she would have me admitted to hospital. There wasn't any real provision for people who were suffering from anorexia at that time, other than admitting them to hospital and tube-feeding them to enable them to gain weight. My family G.P. gave me two alternatives; start eating or be admitted to hospital. The fact that I had to chew mashed potato in order to swallow it, did not bode well on the eating front.

But I was determined that I didn't want to be admitted to hospital.

I started to force-feed myself. Feeling bloated and sick, I chewed each mouthful painfully and slowly. The food would be cold by the time I'd got even halfway through my tiny plateful. I was weak and exhausted, just walking around was an effort, and so undernourished I couldn't think clearly. Life was wearing me out and I was only in my mid-twenties. Each day I persevered and eating became a little easier. I didn't look at myself in the mirror very often, but I noticed that my clothes were starting to fit better. I felt fat, as the pounds piled on.

Having once been so thin and able to feel every bone, it felt strange to have them covered with a cushion of fat. There are lots of theories surrounding anorexia. I think I was too sad and upset to eat. I was grieving the loss of my relationship, my hopes and dreams for the future. I really wanted children of my own but that dream wasn't going to come true for me.

Wearing size twelve clothing when I first became anorexic; I was wearing children's clothes by the time I had lost all the weight. My heart muscle was also affected and I was admitted to Intensive Care on more than one occasion to try to regulate my heart rhythm. Eventually, with lots of help and support, I started to feel better, although I still refused to eat out in public. Most of my battles with the dinner plate were fought in private.

Leaving

Eventually, plucking up the courage to do what needed to be done, I told my husband I wouldn't be home when he returned from work, and that I was leaving him. In response, he said he had heard it all before. This time was different, because I was different. I did leave and I never went back to him. It was a huge relief to finally escape. Enrolling on a teaching training course, having passed an Advanced Diploma in Midwifery, seemed to me the logical next step. As I had always worked in a teaching hospital, I felt that I was quite good at teaching students. I applied for a teaching post in the School of Midwifery, in Sheffield. Never having been to Sheffield before, I was delighted when I was offered the post. Desperate for love and approval, I had become embroiled in another complicated relationship. I kept trying to convince myself that I didn't want commitment and was happy to just "go with the flow." It wasn't true, but I carried on with the relationship for a number of years before I realised it was toxic. At that stage in my life I needed to take care of myself, and not rely on people who couldn't be there for me. The move to Sheffield would be a way of bringing things to a head.

In the August before I moved to Sheffield permanently, my grandmother, whom I loved with all of my heart, died. She was a wise, kind and gentle lady. She had been my sounding board and adviser. I was devastated by her death. Before she died, I sat with her one evening, combing her snow-white hair, she looked up at me and said,

"You make a good nurse Donna."

Of all the commendations and qualifications I have ever received in my life, those are the words I have treasured the most. It was time to make a brand-new start, somewhere, where nobody knew me. I moved to Sheffield that autumn. Packing up all my belongings, and my beloved cat Jess, into my sister's huge, orange, estate car, we set off across the Pennines to Yorkshire. I left in a hurry. There were only four weeks between being offered the teaching post, leaving the maternity unit, and selling the house. I just ran out of time. I didn't even get a chance to say goodbye to friends. It was a big move, but I was travelling light.

As soon as I arrived, I moved into a modern, shared house in Sheffield, which was close to the hospital – the perfect location. A nursing sister was already in residence. She knew lots of people in the area and we became firm friends. She introduced me to her friends which gave me a ready-made social life. Many of them were nurses and rock climbers. Occasionally her brother would come to stay, and I would come home to lots of male students sleeping all over the living room floor.

Most nights, my housemate and I would polish off a bottle of gin between us. Gin became my best friend. I was drinking heavily to blot out what I was feeling. Every morning I woke up hungover and sick. I partied hard. We travelled up and down the country, and most weekends found us in the Peak District, climbing the crags watching others climb and drinking in the local pubs.

At least once a year we would travel down to the South of France, camping and climbing. It was during this time I met a man much younger than me.

He was blonde, blue-eyed, very slim, and tall. He was really funny and different. We didn't think to ask each other how old we were. I was very small and slim, with waist-length auburn hair, and looked much younger than my twenty-nine years. He had a beard, which made him look older, and as his circle of friends was older than him, we both just assumed...

He was lovely, and also very gentle, with the understanding of someone much older. We initially started to see each other as part of the group, but over time, started meeting up together outside of it.

I couldn't say this was an exclusive relationship, but it was fast becoming one. I was accepted into his family from the first day I met them. My housemate bought a house elsewhere, so I moved out and was nearer to his family, in a house of my own. They became a safe haven for me, and a rock when the storms hit.

Glandular fever knocked me off my feet, but instead of getting better over the next few months, I actually got worse. I started picking up infections, barely getting rid of one before I started with something else. Weak, and unable to walk very far, I became a prisoner in my own home. I reached a point where I couldn't even climb the stairs. Exhausted and sick, I employed a home help, and was finally referred to a virologist. I was eventually diagnosed with M.E.

M.E. - "Yuppie Flu"

At that time very little was known about M.E., it was referred to as "yuppie flu." People perceived that it was an illness which wasn't truly 'real', that it was all in the mind. As my physical condition deteriorated, my world shrunk to my living room. The exhaustion was terrible; I felt like I had run several back-to-back marathons. The infections I picked up were bizarre, opportunistic infections, which had me bedridden for much of the time. I suffered from cold sores, which covered one entire side of my face and went inside my eye. I realised during that time how it must feel to have some sort of physical deformity. People would openly stare at me in public. I looked as though I had been battered, and my eye remained half closed. Unable to go to work full-time, I cut my hours down to part-time in an effort to keep working.

I had difficulty reading and retaining information because of 'brain fog'; not a good thing to happen to a lecturer. The virologist was concerned I might be suffering from HIV, so I had the nightmare of waiting for the test results to come back, which thankfully were negative. I felt I had got off lightly.

Slowly I started to improve, but it took years of help and care to start to feel anything like normal. As more became known about the condition, Myalgic Encephalomyelitis I and many others were able to improve our situations. I was so blessed I was able to come through, as so many others do not always improve or get better. Even today my body does not fight off infections easily, and I still suffer times of complete exhaustion.

Depression

All this took a toll on my relationship. At first the age gap didn't seem to matter, but gradually we began to want, and need, very different things. Inevitably, despite still caring about each other, we went our separate ways and I found myself alone in my mid-thirties. I had no family of my own, was physically fragile, and sliding deeper into depression. One day, in a fit of self-loathing, I went to the hairdresser's and had all my long red hair cut off. The hairdresser was really reluctant to do something so drastic but I was adamant. I watched as she dropped lengths of my hair into a basket. When she had finished, it was really short; I looked almost boyish. When I got home, I looked in the mirror for a long time at the new me, then burst into tears.

Alcoholics Anonymous (Al Anon)

I had been reading a book called "Women Who Love Too Much", by a woman called Robin Norwood. She was writing about the adult children of alcoholics, and adult co-dependency. She described co-dependency, and the behavioural traits of children growing up in that type of environment, and adults living co-dependently with addicts. As I continued to read, something clicked. She mentioned an Organisation for family and friends of alcoholics, called Alcoholics Anonymous (Al Anon). Anyone can attend Al Anon, even if the alcoholic refuses to attend. This woman was describing me. I finished the book and that same evening I attended my first meeting. It felt scary but wonderful, to be in a room with people who felt and behaved exactly as I did. They had been where I had been and had come out the other side.

Al Anon is not a place to slag off the alcoholic in your life, but a place to keep the focus on yourself and your crazy co-dependent behaviour. There were men and women there who no longer lived with the addict in their family but came to meetings to keep them sane.

Being in a co-dependent relationship is the sure way to insanity. Always focusing on the addict, there is no time to focus on yourself or your needs. I constantly reacted to people. My behaviour could be completely over the top, shouting and screaming, or withdrawn and anxious. Not having had a life of my own, I had always been in relationships with people who took up all of my time and effort. I knew that my behaviour was not always sane or coherent, and despised myself for sitting around waiting for the men in my life. I didn't know what I liked or who I really was. I was like a chameleon, taking on the colour of the latest person I was with. I had completely lost my sense of self, if I had ever had it to begin with.

For me, Al Anon was a lifeline. I had tried going to a church, but I wasn't really ready for that. Taking anti-depressants and seeing a therapist had helped a little, but working the Twelve Steps of Al Anon helped me to process my own feelings and behaviour. It helped me to take the focus off others and find out who I really was. Up to that point in my life, I don't think I had ever taken the time to really think about what I liked or wanted. I had always been in a situation where my wants and needs were secondary to the person I was with. If you had asked me then what music I liked, or where I liked to go, or what I enjoyed doing I wouldn't have been able to tell you. I didn't actually know what I liked and disliked. For me, the Twelve Step Al Anon meetings were transformational, and the fact that the Twelve Steps had a spiritual core, set me on a path towards the God I had rejected, because I thought He had rejected me.

Starting Over ... Again

In the Summer of 1996 my sister invited me to a house party. A friend of her husband's was there and she introduced me to him. He seemed like a nice guy, I spent most of the evening talking to him. He lived down South but was originally from the North. We started to see each other at weekends. He would come to Sheffield or I would go to him. We got on well and enjoyed being in each other's company. Before long, he decided he wanted to move back to the North-West.

He got a new job and we decided to live together. I would move from Sheffield to a house we had found in Glossop, in the High Peak. It was an emotional wrench leaving Sheffield after ten years. I loved my little terraced house. I had spent a lot of time and money renovating it and making it perfect for me. I had put down roots and made good friends there, but Glossop beckoned. It wasn't too far away, so I could still keep in touch, but yet again, I found myself moving on and starting over.

It was strange to be living in a small town, after living in a large city. We shared our beautiful home with two cats and a border collie. It was a renovated schoolhouse, which had been given two floors. The top floor had the most amazing, huge, carved cornices. The back bedroom window overlooked the converted chapel next door. I could see the enormous stained-glass window, with Jesus, arms wide open, staring back at me. It felt comforting to think that He might be reaching out but it also made me sad. I knew that my life was very far from the plans He might have had for me. Some days I couldn't bear to look at His concerned face gazing my way.

Dabbling in the Occult

Mediums and clairvoyants fascinated me, not least because I appeared to have a similar gift. I remember playing with Ouija boards; we tried it one night when I worked at the hospital. I didn't believe it was true, I thought the others were pushing the glass and trying to spook me. So they took their fingers off the glass, leaving only mine, and the glass spelled out, "Donna is my medium." I was completely freaked out. Something else which really grabbed my attention, was automatic writing.

One of the mediums I had consulted, told me to ask my 'spirit guide' what its name was the next time I sat down to write. Alone in the house one evening, I picked up my pen and paper and began.

Holding the pen to the paper, my hand started to move across the page. I then asked my 'spirit guide' its name. I was expecting a Native American – isn't that what always comes through or perhaps Marie Antoinette, if you are lucky? What the 'spirit' wrote on my page caused me to break out in a cold sweat. I looked in horror as my own hand spelled out SATAN on the page. Not wanting to believe my own eyes I asked again. Again, S A T A N was carefully spelled out across the page.

Throwing the writing pad down I ran upstairs to the sitting room, fighting to keep calm.

What happened next literally had my hair standing on end. The static electricity in the room increased, until even the hairs on my arms were standing up. Turning towards the door I saw a figure in the doorway, yet it was somehow bigger than the doorway itself. There was a black void where its face should have been. Vivid flashes of light surrounded the figure, which was terrifying. The light bulbs in the room and on the landing grew brighter and brighter, as if there was some sort of power surge.

Then they suddenly shattered into a thousand pieces, leaving me in complete darkness.

There was an electrical burning smell, and shards of glass covered the carpet. No matter, I was on my knees. The glass cut into my flesh, but I didn't care because I was too busy promising God that I would never, ever do that again. The room became quiet except for the banging of my heart against my ribcage and in my ears, I had broken out in a cold sweat. It was one of the most terrifying experiences of my life, and it cured my curiosity with mediums and spirits for good.

July 1999 – A Stroke

During July 1999 I was staying with a friend for the weekend. Already packed and ready to leave on the Sunday we decided to have a coffee before I set off for the long drive home to Glossop. Leaning forward to pick up the mug, disturbingly, I could see two mugs in front of me. Looking up, I could see two of everything. Rubbing my eyes didn't help. I opened my mouth to speak.

My tongue was twisted, as I felt my mouth turn down and my eyelid droop. My right arm became heavier and heavier, followed by a similar feeling in my leg. It felt like dominoes being knocked over, one by one, in rapid succession. Strangely, I didn't panic. Totally shocked that this was actually happening to me, I managed to blurt out,

"I think I'm having a stroke," before my body hit the floor hard.

My friend remained really calm and dialled 999. Miraculously, within a few minutes an ambulance had arrived and an oxygen mask was covering my face. I had double vision; I was trying to speak, but the words kept coming out wrong. I couldn't locate my tongue in my mouth and I was drooling like a baby. I will be forever grateful for the prompt treatment I received that day. I have no doubt that it saved millions of brain cells and gave me the very best chance of recovery.

The double vision thankfully resolved fairly quickly. Not so my swallowing reflex, or the paralysis of my right side. My hand and foot felt ten times larger than they actually were. All my fingers felt fat, like a rubber glove blown up with air. I couldn't hold anything or pick anything up.

My speech was slow and slurred. To this day I still have right-sided weakness, and I have had to learn to balance on the inside of my right foot, in order to walk or stay upright. As if all of this was not bad enough, no one prepared me for the 'aftershocks.'

Following a brain injury, the brain swells. To me it felt as though someone was hitting the inside of my head with a lump hammer. I could hear the metallic thud-thud-thud on the inside of my skull. This happened frequently in the first few weeks. The waves of nausea which accompanied it were awful. It was a wretched and terrifying time. I did a lot of praying. Someone told me God was always listening. This would be in sharp contrast to the man I was living with, who didn't make it to my bedside until thirty-six hours later. I spent my forty-first birthday alone and frightened, in a hospital bed many miles away from home. It is said that sometimes a little knowledge can be a bad

thing, and so it proved to be. Terrified at the thought of remaining partially paralysed, permanently, my anxiety levels were off the scale.

My physiotherapist was fantastic, she helped me to regain better movement in my hand and arm. I couldn't perform fine motor movements or use a knife and fork. I also had to learn to walk without overbalancing. It was a really long process, but with her help I began to improve. Even though daily tasks took ten times longer to perform, I always tried to use my right hand, in the hope that new nerve pathways would be formed in my brain. I quit my twenty cigarettes a day habit and focused on recovery.

Once settled back at home, I continued my search for all things spiritual, including a Buddhist meditation group, and New Age practices and practitioners. I tried to steer clear of mediums, which still held some fascination. Yet in all of my spiritual seeking, I was being drawn back time after time to the person of Jesus. As much as I resisted the pull, the urge became stronger. Sitting in a Buddhist meditation session one evening the thought came into my head.

"I believe in Jesus."

It was as simple and as stark as that. I made my apologies and left the room. I felt bad for just walking out but I knew deep down it wasn't the place for me.

CHAPTER SIX

A New Millenium

The eve of the new Millennium and I was spending the night at home with my mum. Whilst parties and fireworks were in full swing, we were sat watching Jools Holland and assorted guests, 'Hootenanny' their way into the next thousand years.

Most of my family and friends worked in the NHS as nurse managers. They had all been drafted into the hospitals overnight to help defend against "the collapse of civilisation", when the Y2K bug hit at midnight. As it happened, the NHS spent large sums of money paying senior managers to do the night shift. Poised and ready for 'NHS Armageddon,' the clock struck midnight and … absolutely nothing happened. Whatever the cyber geeks had done to avert disaster, amazingly, had worked, and so one of the nation's most treasured institutions was saved. It turned out that January 1st 2000 looked, and felt, very much like 31st December 1999. All the problems of the previous year had been dragged into another century along with us. It was to get much worse for me over the next few months.

Hemiplegic Migraine, (H.M.)

Still struggling with the effects of the stroke I had suffered the previous summer, I had mobility problems and struggled with dexterity. I now also suffered from Hemiplegic migraine (H.M.), a rare condition, which causes aura symptoms of migraine, along with weakness and paralysis of the face and limbs. The attacks happened with alarming frequency, and nothing the doctors prescribed was able to bring them under control. The attacks were terrifying. They usually started with visual disturbance followed by numbness of the tongue, face and throat, thereafter, followed by weakness or paralysis of my right arm and leg. Eventually, the neurologist caring for me concluded that rather than the stroke causing the hemiplegic migraine, it was probably the other way around. I learned a lot about it over the next few years.

Only 1-2% of people suffering from migraine have H.M. It may or may not be genetic.

Treatment is still pretty much trial and error. I became a guinea pig for many different drugs, most of them used in epilepsy. To anyone suffering from migraine, I can only say, go to your G.P. and get a diagnosis and treatment. Migraine is not just a headache. It is much more serious and shouldn't be passed off as a common stress headache. I ignored my migraine attacks and paid a heavy price.

I couldn't bear bright lights or fast-moving objects. They made me feel nauseous and dizzy. The right side of my face still felt solid, like wood. I had difficulty swallowing, but my motor skills were improving. Walking was slow but I could walk alright with a walking stick. I had had to give up my work as a midwifery teacher; my poor brain wasn't up to reading or thinking too much. I couldn't read, watch TV, or go on long walks as I used to. I felt helpless and useless. I was medically retired and on the scrap heap in my early forties.

If I was fearful about my future, my 'then' partner was struggling also, with the fact that overnight I had become dependent, physically and financially. In short, I realised that in his eyes I was probably becoming a burden. Our relationship started to unravel and my life began to slide into chaos. Not for the first time, I was in free-fall, without a clue as to where I would land.

Easter 2000 - Coming Home

Just before Easter I suffered a mini stroke, or transient Ischaemic attack and was rushed to the local hospital for tests and observation. I was given a lumbar puncture; something I had seen done to others, but had never had done to me. I have to say I wish I had been much more sympathetic to patients undergoing the procedure in the past.

I felt really lonely, sad and scared.

As I lay in that hospital bed, for the best part of a week, it gave me lots of time to think about my life and where it was heading. My life had been so varied and fast moving for so many years, it was the first time I had really given serious thought to what I was doing in my life. Some things weighed heavy on my mind and I had frequent nightmares. I asked the Sister in charge of the ward, if I could get to see the hospital chaplain or a Catholic Priest. I don't know why I asked, but somehow, I felt that talking to someone like that might make me feel better. I'm not sure if she passed the message on or not, but the chaplain never materialised. I concluded that God, if He even existed, had definitely turned His back on me.

A lady called Elsie was in one of the side wards. I could see her room from my bed. Every day she came to talk to me and others on the main ward, leaving little gifts and books. Elsie had lots of visitors, including lots of young people. Her little room was full of laughter, chatter and singing. It made me curious as to what was going on and who all these people were.

Eventually I plucked up the courage to venture into this little oasis in my parched desert. Lying on Elsie's bed, I would listen to everyone talking; they all seemed so happy. Being with Elsie and her friends did my heart good.

I spoke to Elsie about my feelings. I had been brought up in the Roman Catholic tradition. I would have said that I knew about Jesus, and I loved going to church as a child. I went there to escape. I told Elsie that I had turned my back on God, like many before me I felt hurt, and blamed God for all my problems, when the reality was, I was the one at fault. I was longing to get closer to Him; I just didn't know how.

Night times on the ward were the worst. Trying to sleep in that long Nightingale ward was almost impossible, with or without medication. The nurses sat around a table in the centre of the ward. Seemingly incapable of talking quietly, they carried on their conversations as though it was the middle of the day. I was so irritated. The telephone rang loudly and regularly. It was completely exhausting. Thirty bodies tossed and turned like ships in a storm. The plastic mattresses made you sweat. After a long night of broken sleep, the nurses would cheerfully switch on the main lights and 'wake us up.' Not having actually slept, we dutifully sat up without complaint, whilst the nurses bustled about washing faces, and feeding us with lukewarm tea and soggy toast. By 1 p.m. everyone would be snoring loudly, trying to catch up on lost sleep in an attempt to keep insanity at bay.

Despite my request, I still hadn't met anyone remotely priest-like. Elsie asked if I would like to speak to her pastor, whose name was Tim. He was visiting with her that afternoon. Later that day a young man in ordinary clothes came to sit by my bed. He introduced himself, and what followed next was, to me, extraordinary. He prayed for me and as he prayed I felt a peace come over me unlike I had ever felt before. What I didn't know, was that he was praying in the power of the Holy Spirit. He told me about a church in Glossop with a really good vicar. He suggested I go along when I got home.

Soon after that meeting, the Consultant decided I was well enough to be discharged from the ward. I said my goodbyes to Elsie, promising to keep in touch. I did so, until her husband Derek contacted me some months later to tell me that Elsie had died peacefully in the hospice. I was so sad. I will always remember her as a beautiful, Holy Spirit-filled lady, who radiated love and had a massive heart, for 'hurting people', like me. I am totally sure that I will see her again one day in heaven.

Home. It should have felt comfortable and safe, but instead, my partner spent longer periods of time away from me. I would stay in the bedroom for hours during the day, accompanied by my two cats and our collie dog. They would be lying all around me on the bed, staring at me with a concerned look in their eyes. I was really blessed by the love of those animals. It was totally faithful and unconditional. They comforted me when I needed it the most.

Easter was on the horizon. Someone from Whitfield Parish had posted a card through the door advertising their Easter services. On Maundy Thursday, at St James' Church they were having a meal commemorating the 'Last Supper' Jesus had with His disciples. I decided to go, mostly out of curiosity. The first person I met was a lovely lady called Minnie. She gladly took me under her wing and sat beside me for the whole evening. Everyone was so welcoming and friendly. Colin, the Vicar and his wife Linda, were really lovely, genuine people. It was strange at first, sitting sharing a meal with all these people I had only just met, but I felt secure and safe in that room.

Having stepped out of my comfort zone, on the following day, Good Friday, I decided to go to church again. I had been reading the book, 'The Jesus I Never Knew' by Philip Yancey, which was a real eye-opener for me and made me want to know this Jesus better. That morning I set off slowly with my new must-have accessory, a walking stick in the shape of a shepherd's crook. On reaching the end of the street, I could see St. Luke's church in front of me.

I had been there once before but I had already decided that having been brought up as a Catholic, I should probably go to a Catholic church. Truth was, as a Roman Catholic, despite decades of ecumenical endeavour at that time, it felt wrong to go to a "protestant" church. It was ingrained in me that any other church was to be avoided.

Drawing level with St. Luke's, something amazing happened. I heard an actual voice, so clearly it stopped me in my tracks and made me turn around to see who was speaking. The voice was quite clear and very calm.

"Donna, I want you to go to St. Luke's today."

Rooted to the spot, thinking I might be going mad, I answered back.

"I'm sorry?" I said to the air around me.

"I don't want you to go to St Mary's today; I want you to go to St. Luke's."

"Is this God?"

"Yes, and I want you to go to St. Luke's".

Speechless, I stood in the middle of the footpath. What to do? I reasoned that if this was in fact God Himself, then I had better do as He said. You may question my sanity at this point, but I was compelled to go into that church. I walked very slowly up the path to the door. Once inside St. Luke's, the welcome I received was overwhelming. I felt like I had finally come home.

Colin who was the vicar of both St Lukes' and St James' came to speak to me. I told him I thought that God had told me to come into the church. Without a flicker of doubt in his voice, he said,

"Well in that case, you had better come in."

I did just that. A dear lady I had met twelve months before approached me, and greeted me with a lovely smile. She even remembered my name. I can't tell you how welcome that lady recollecting me, made me feel. The fact that she had even remembered my face, let alone my name, amazed and humbled me. Since that day I have been in numerous churches, and some of the warmest welcomes have come from the smallest and humblest of congregations. Welcoming someone into church is so important. It takes courage to walk into a church building filled with people they don't know and a place that has its own rituals and language.

That Easter was a revelation to me. I missed the smells and bells of the Roman Catholic ritual, but the difference in this church was the sheer level of joy I experienced. Everyone seemed to be truly delighted to be there. I went to all the Easter services and felt a pull on my heart, so strong I couldn't ignore it. My partner was bemused at first by my sudden 'religious' fervour, but to me this wasn't religion. He probably saw it as a hobby, like the embroidery and tapestries I had taken up to help improve my hand co-ordination.

Alpha Course

Just after Easter 2000, the church was holding an Alpha Course. Alpha was designed by Nicky Gumbel, a pastor at Holy Trinity, Brompton, in London. It was designed to help people to understand and experience the Christian faith, in an informal and relaxed way. I decided to put my name down; it couldn't hurt to find out more about Jesus (who seemed to be working His way back into my life]. Alpha was great. It was held in the home of Adele and Dave, who became good friends, along with their children, Alison, Lizzie, Joy and James.

At each Alpha evening we shared a meal and listened to a short talk, followed by an opportunity to ask questions, in a small group. I realised there was so much I actually didn't know about Jesus, or the Bible in general. By the end of the course, I was asked if I wanted to ask Jesus into my life, to be my Saviour. This confused me, because I thought as I had been baptised, I didn't really have to "ask Him into my life." It was explained to me that since I had been a baby when I was baptised, promises had been made to God on my behalf, by my parents and godparents. Now as an adult, I had the opportunity to choose to follow God myself; to say sorry for the things I had done wrong and to turn to Him. So I did. I received Jesus Christ as my personal Lord and Saviour the most defining decision I've ever made.

From that moment my world changed. Like my friend Gill said, it was as though I had been watching black and white TV for years, then suddenly changed to a colour set. Everything seemed brand new. I had a new beginning. Creation and colour dazzled me with its beauty, its brightness and its clarity. I came to realise that talking about the Holy Spirit was a very different thing to having Him with you and within you. I opened my heart and He rocked my world.

With this new-found clarity came unexpected problems, because the more I grew in faith, my view of things was changing. I began to see what was wrong in my relationship with my partner. At first, he really encouraged me to go to church and to get involved. But as the year wore on, things started to go wrong. I told him I thought that if we were going to carry on living together, we should get married. We had been together for five years and had announced our engagement some two years before. One evening as we were talking about what to do next, he told me he had something to say. That 'something' was that he didn't want to get married. He didn't know why but he felt that we should call an end to our relationship. I was devastated. It was the week before Christmas. Why couldn't he have said all this sooner?

Christmas was miserable. I felt abandoned and so angry. I cried for days. How could he just cast me off like an old coat? Leaving a relationship is never simple. When you have been that close to someone, when they leave, it is like trying to peel apart two pieces of paper which have been glued together. No matter how you try, the pages won't come apart cleanly; a bit of one page is always firmly stuck to the other and vice versa. I was sad to lose our collie who had been so faithful and to lose my partner's Mum who I had become very fond of. My Dad, who was not often given to sentiment, expressing his feelings or giving advice, was clear when he said,

> "He doesn't deserve you, there is a much better man out there for you."

I didn't agree, at least not then. To be honest, I didn't want another relationship. I was done with men.

It was March 2001 before the house I shared with my now ex-partner was sold. I managed to buy a tiny, two-bedroomed cottage, which was just a few steps from the Lych gate of St. James' church. It felt comforting to be living so close to, what was fast becoming, my home church. I finally moved in, just before Easter of that year. There seemed to be a pattern emerging. These Easter milestones served to remind me of the new life I had embarked on.

Friends helped me to decorate the new place and move my few pieces of furniture, and zillions of books, into my new home. The house was tiny, but it was fine for me, besides, I had no intention of sharing it with anyone else. Emotionally battered, I was thankful for a fresh start. The back garden was pretty, and shared with two other properties. Forty-four, and single yet again, I sat in my new home and had a long chat with God. That is, I talked and He listened.

"That's it. No more men. From now on it's just you and me."

I meant every word I said.

God had other ideas.

September 2001

Six months after moving I was settling into my new life. At first I hated living alone and continually sought out company. But eventually I started to like, and value, my own space. Browsing through the local paper one evening, I saw an advert for a coach trip to Paris. It was a four-night break, travelling by coach and ferry. The ferry bit concerned me because of my seasickness, but it was reasonably priced and looked interesting. The only thing was, who to go with? I asked my mum if she fancied the trip. After all, no one else was going to take us. She was delighted to be asked, so I booked our places, and began making preparations for what turned out to be a really big adventure, which would turn my world upside down and shake it to its very foundations.

CHAPTER SEVEN

Paris

Paris, the most romantic city on the planet. Our day started at four a.m. Not being a 'morning person,' dragging myself out from under the duvet was a feat in itself. Mum and I trundled our luggage through the deserted, rain-soaked streets of Glossop, to the waiting coach. It was huge. The driver informed us that we would be making numerous stops en-route to pick up other passengers. We went to the rear of the coach and settled into our seats ready for the long journey South.

Around five a.m. we reached Eccles, in Salford, stopping to pick up four passengers, three men and a woman. I assumed that one of the men, and the woman, were acting as carers for the other two. The tallest man sat at the front of the coach, folding his long frame into the narrow seat. I noticed that he sat with his legs stretched out into the aisle. As we continued on, the mumble of conversation grew louder as people started to introduce themselves to one another.

I turned my attention to those sitting around me. There were several couples, most of them older than me, and a few singletons dotted about the coach. I began to wonder what was drawing all of us to Paris. It seemed to me at the time, that travelling alone to Paris was like sitting in front of the Taj Mahal by yourself. The much-published picture of the late Princess Diana, sitting in a solitary pose at the Taj Mahal in India, came to mind.

After a long journey, punctuated by numerous stops and seemingly endless miles of motorway, we finally arrived at Dover. Once on board the ferry, I lost sight of the little group from the front of the coach. The crossing was not smooth. It reminded me of the times as a child, I used to travel on the ferry to Ireland to see my granny. Genetics counted for nothing as far as sailing was concerned. I was a very bad sailor. My dad, who was a bosun (a non-commissioned officer) in the Merchant Navy, had to suffer the shame of his young daughter throwing up in the aisles of the ferry from Holyhead to Dublin! As we set off for Calais, I made the decision to look back. I focused on the chalk line of the white cliffs of Dover, underlining the coast of England, rather than watch the port of Calais heaving into view. It proved to be a successful strategy. I didn't throw up.

Arriving at Calais we boarded the coach, which whisked us off towards Paris. It was rush hour, French style. We drove around the Boulevard Peripherique at a snail's pace. It was just like driving on the M25, with French subtitles. Finally, in the late evening we arrived at our hotel. Tired and hungry, we queued at reception to book into our rooms. I stood behind the tall guy from the coach, noticing his hair, which gathered in soft silvery curls at the nape of his neck. There was only time for a quick snack and then some welcome sleep. I fell asleep, putting the man and his curls firmly out of my mind.

We woke early, in time for breakfast. The man with the curls was sitting at a nearby table, wearing a t-shirt, and a pair of shorts that were showing off his long, tanned legs. I concentrated on my breakfast. The coach was ready to take us to the Palace at Versailles. This time I boarded the coach from the front door. The tall man with curls was sitting at the front. I smiled at him. He smiled back. It was a smile that could light up a room. He was gorgeous, with the bluest eyes and the whitest teeth. Making my way to the back of the coach I could feel his eyes on me. As we set off, I was aware he kept looking back at me. Doing my best to ignore him, I couldn't help but glance in his direction.

The Palace at Versailles was amazing. It is the most beautiful, eighteenth-century Chateau, commissioned by the Sun King, Louis XIII. The Hall of Mirrors, the most famous room in the palace, was totally jaw-dropping. Its three hundred and seventy-five mirrors reflected light from the windows, and from the huge chandeliers that hung from the ceiling and ran the length of the hall. Marie Antoinette's bedchamber was equally lavish. It housed a tiny bed with an ornate canopy and tassels, and swags of material which fell from ceiling to floor. Everything was gilded in gold and decorated with flowers. I longed to step over the gold rail, that kept you from touching it, and hurl myself onto that bed with its plump cushions.

The tour of the Chateau over, we were given an hour to get a snack in one of the nearby cafes and bars. Mum and I sat in the front window of one of the cafes. I soon became aware that the man from the coach was in the next room. He kept looking over to us. Blushing like a teenager; I put my head down trying not to look back.

From Versailles we were driven to Notre Dame Cathedral, and then were allowed to make our own way back to the hotel. I ate with mum that afternoon, in one of the small restaurants nearby.

Both of us were shocked to see customers eating lunch with their pet dogs sitting on the tables, being fed from the owner's plate. We were even more astounded to see that the restaurant owners allowed them to do so! We discovered there is no city in the world that treats its dogs as well as they do in Paris. It seemed as though every other person was a dog owner. French people are permitted to take their pets into places usually frowned upon in the U.K. However, they are not allowed into the many parks, or pristine gardens, around the city. There are small green machines constantly being driven on the pavements to clear up any dog mess left behind.

Exhausted from the early start and the miles of walking around the city, we made it back to the hotel, but there was little time to rest. That evening we were being taken on a tour of Paris by night. The Millennium lights were still in place. It promised to be a stunning evening.

Boarding our coach once more, we set off into the Parisian evening, driving by the Moulin Rouge and its famous windmill, the beautiful Sacre Coeur and around the Arc de Triomphe competing with the hundreds of vehicles and blaring horns. Eventually, the coach came to a halt at the end of a long mall, where we disembarked to walk to the base of the Eiffel Tower. No ordinary tower, this.

It is one of the most iconic towers ever built. Modelled, photographed and painted by millions of people for over a century, I had seen countless images of this tower, but nothing had prepared me to see it up close.

There were jugglers and acrobats dressed in silver costumes, which sparkled and dazzled in the lights at the base. Overhead, thousands of lights adorning the tower twinkled and shone with an intensity you could barely look at. A huge searchlight shone out across the city from the very top of the tower. As I stopped to take a picture of the breath-taking scene, I heard a voice behind me.

"Would you like me to take a picture of you both?"

I turned to see who had spoken and looked up into the bluest eyes imaginable. Mumbling my thanks I handed him the camera. He took the picture, then walked with us to the base of the tower. From the moment we met, it was as though we had known each other for ever. He had a smile that made me melt. Greyish-blonde hair with soft curls, and dressed in smart casual clothes. I recognised a Mancunian dialect overlaying a Midlands accent. He introduced himself as Nick.

Walking back to the coach, he asked if I would like to go out for a drink when we returned to the hotel.

"Just me?" I asked, feeling more than a little bit flustered.

"Well yes, I think so." He looked amused.

"I'm sorry, I'll have to let my mum know, I'm travelling with her you see…"

My voice trailed. I must have looked like an over-ripe tomato squashed on a plate. This was more than a hormonal hot flush.

Back on the coach I broached the subject with mum.

"Mum, that man sitting at the front has just asked me to go for a drink with him".

"Who is he?" Mum said, with a tone of alarm in her voice.

"I don't know, I've only just met him".

She wasn't impressed.

"Well. It's up to you, if you want to go with him. I'll go back to the hotel and get an early night."

I kissed her.

"Thanks Mum."

"Don't be late back; we've got a trip on the boat tomorrow."

"I promise." I lied, making a promise I couldn't keep. "Thanks Mum."

We arrived back at the hotel around 10.30 p.m. Nick and I said goodnight to our fellow travelers and set off into the streets of Paris. Given that he had made the first move, he suddenly seemed really shy. I cautiously took hold of his hand as we walked along. It was a warm night, and the streets were lined with chestnut trees. Stopping at a small cafe bar, we sat out on the terrace overlooking the street and started to talk and talk and talk. He told me he and his wife had split up some time ago, and that he had children. When he told me he had five children, I nearly fell off my chair. Sadly, apart from the eldest, he hadn't seen them for a long time.

I learned that he was from Coventry and loved his football club, Coventry City F.C. In fact, following the team up and down the country was something of an obsession for him. He had worked in banks and building societies, here and abroad, and had moved up North when he was only seventeen. I asked about the people he was travelling with. It turned out the lady was called Lillian and was a support worker. Like Nick, the other two guys were clients. He proceeded to tell me that he had had a mental breakdown a few years before and had been in a psychiatric hospital for more than six months. He was in recovery now and working for Age UK, and was living in a ten- bedroomed house near Monton.

My mind was reeling trying to take in all this information. I was attempting to work out what had happened to him, to warrant such a lengthy time in a psychiatric hospital, and what he was doing with Lillian and the other two men. What was I getting myself into? We had no idea of the time. The waiters kept filling our glasses. The wine was flowing and no one seemed to be in a hurry to ask us to leave.

I told him I had been divorced from my husband for some time, and had

had a few long-term relationships which had come to nothing and generally ended painfully. I told him I had been a nurse and midwifery teacher, and had been working in Lancashire and Yorkshire. I had no children of my own, despite delivering hundreds of babies for others. That I had recently suffered a stroke and was recovering well.

So far so good, but a warning bell was clanging in the back of my mind. I ignored it. Fascinated now by this man, I wanted to get to know him better.

My promise to Mum, to be back early, was well and truly broken. By the time Nick and I walked back to the hotel through the now deserted streets, it was already four in the morning. An early morning dew had settled on the Chestnut trees lining the boulevards. The birds were just beginning their dawn chorus. We had to knock at the hotel door to alert the night porter, who opened the door, bleary eyed and giving us a sly wink. Creeping quietly up the stairs, stopping every so often to prolong the evening, we were giggling like two big kids. Arriving at my bedroom door I attempted to push the key card into the lock, without success. Numerous attempts later we were helpless with laughter. That is, until the door suddenly flew open and Mum stood there.

"Where the hell have you been? Do you know what time it is? I've been worried sick about you."

I tried to blag my way in, telling mum we had lost track of time. I pointed out that I wasn't exactly a teenager.

Mum continued,

> "Well you had better be up in the morning; we have to be on the coach to Montmartre for nine o' clock."

I promised I would be up. I reckoned that gave me three to four hours sleep if I was lucky.

Looking back I can't believe I was so thoughtless. Looking at it from Mum's point of view, I was in a foreign city in the middle of the night with a man I had only just met, and with no way of contacting her.

Where was Nick? You may well ask. He had run up the stairs the moment Mum opened the door. To be fair, I didn't blame him. However, if he thought he was getting off lightly, he was wrong.

Mum hadn't finished with him yet.

The next two days were amazing. We went to Montmartre, where through half-closed eyes we watched artists of every kind going about their work. There were portrait and landscape painters, and living statues so realistic you really did have to look twice at them. Sacre Coeur was as beautiful inside, as out. From the door of the Basilica we could see the whole of Paris stretched out before us, like a patchwork quilt drying in the noonday sun. Cafes and bars were alive with music and the aroma of delicious food. The chatter of conversation could be heard in dozens of languages.

We travelled on a Baton Mouche – a pleasure boat, which travelled up and down the length of the River Seine. Mum bravely rode shotgun, and we laughed and laughed as the commentator explained the different landmarks as we floated passed them. The problem was that by the time he got to the English translation we had moved on to the next landmark, and so we were always one behind and on our way to the next tourist spot.

Having met Lillian and the other two lads during the course of the day, we decided we should all meet up for dinner later, at the interestingly named 'Hippopotamus' restaurant. They served simple foods, like steak and frites It was also inexpensive, which was perfect for us. Before we set off for the evening, Nick came to our room. He handed me a single red rose and a beautiful silver cross and chain, which he had bought in Notre dame Cathedral. Mum looked at the gifts.

"He means business," she said sourly.

"Hmm, he does, doesn't he?"

"Have you told him yet that you're a Christian and you go to church?"

"No not yet."

"Don't you think you should tell him before things go any further?"

"It's not like I'm going to marry him" I retorted.

I agreed with Mum, but didn't know how I was going to bring the subject up without alarming Nick or putting him off. Inside I was panicking and praying. "Please God give me the chance to tell him, but let it be spontaneous." Putting the cross and chain around my neck, I was finally ready. We set off to the restaurant.

It was a good evening; everyone was getting on well. There were eight of us around the table. Nick sat next to me and further down the table sat 'T.' He was so tiny; a lovely man who had come with Nick and was sharing his room. Out of the blue, halfway through the meal, T asked me a question.

"Donna, are you a Christian?"

I was taken aback, and flustered.

"Yes, I am. What makes you ask that?"

"You're wearing a cross," he answered simply.

Everyone's eyes were agog, waiting for me to give an answer. I explained to the whole table (and anyone else who was listening) that I was a Christian, and that my faith wasn't just for Sundays. It was a life choice, and I tried to live my life as best I could as a follower of Jesus. I could feel Nick's eyes boring into me, but I didn't look sideways, so I couldn't see the expression on his face. T's curiosity satisfied, we went back to eating our meal and talking about the day's events. On our way back to the hotel, Nick asked if going to church would do him any good. I said it wouldn't do him any harm, and there the matter rested for the time being.

The next day we packed up, ready for the long drive home. Our time in Paris was over. I was certain we would see each other again and didn't want this bubble to burst.

Once on the ferry I headed for the duty free. Nick sat with my mum in the lounge. I learned later that she gave him the low-down on what she expected. She told him I had been through some horrendous times and she didn't want to see me get hurt again. This time it was Nick's turn to make a promise he wouldn't be able to keep.

We sat together all the way home, on the back seat. Everyone on the coach was now aware of the budding romance. We laughed all the way, even as we were passing through the Battle of the Somme landmark, which brought disapproving looks and hard stares from my Mum and other passengers. When the time came for Nick to get off the coach, I was devastated. As much as I told myself I had only just met him, that I was being ridiculous, I couldn't stop myself from crying. I waved from the back window until he was completely out of sight.

Mum stayed with me that night. We had a lie-in the following morning as both of us were exhausted by the journey. On waking, I made breakfast and switched on the TV. Instead of the usual morning television, there were images of the World Trade Centre in the USA. One of the Twin Towers was on fire. It seemed that a tragic accident had happened involving a commercial passenger plane. The images were shocking. Flames were pouring out of the building. Tons of paper fluttered like giant confetti in the smoke-filled sky. People were hanging out of windows, desperately waving tablecloths or clothing, whatever they could lay their hands on. As we watched this grim scene a second plane came into view, ploughing into the second Tower. It was such a shocking image and definitely no accident. Breakfast forgotten, we sat speechless, watching the scenes on the screen in front of us. A minute later the phone rang. It was Nick.

"Are you watching this?"

On so many levels, our world was never going to be the same again.

PART THREE

NICK &
DONNA

CHAPTER EIGHT

After Paris

A few days after we returned from Paris, we were both walking on clouds. Nick's birthday was on the 13th of September, so I told him I would treat him to tapas in Manchester. We met on Piccadilly station, surrounded by the rush of commuters running for trains. It was as though we had never been apart. The evening went by far too fast. We picked up where we left off and carried on chatting for the rest of the evening.

Soon after, Nick introduced me to the residents of the house on Wellington Road. They were all lovely people and welcomed me into their world. There were some very vulnerable people living there, and the fact that they were willing to trust me was such an honour. He took me to meet his co-workers at Age Concern (now Age UK), who seemed to be genuinely happy that Nick had met someone. Everything was moving so quickly I hardly had time to think. Yet it seemed so natural to be with him. Still, there was something I couldn't quite put my finger on. I could see that he wasn't a drinker or a smoker and there wasn't any evidence of drug use. Nick started attending my home church on Sundays. Everyone was welcoming, and he really did seem to enjoy being there. I realised that the main reason he was coming to church was to spend more time with me, but gradually he started to listen to what was being said and came to the conclusion that it might be for him too. The minister asked how I was. I had told him about Nick, and I was obviously smitten, and then he asked THE question.

"Is Nick a Christian?"

I surprised myself with my reply.

"No, he isn't, but he is going to be because we are going to pray for him."

Colin didn't look as sure as I felt, but I firmly believed every word I'd said.

At the beginning of October, the church was having a weekend away. Nick said that he would stay at my place to look after my two cats and do some painting. In the evenings he would be able to see my friends, Adele and David, so he wouldn't be too lonely. It was during that weekend that Nick asked Jesus into his life. He told me over the phone. I thought my heart would burst with joy. I knew that if our relationship was going to go any further, it was important that we had a shared faith. As lovely as Nick was, he would have to share my faith because it was such a huge part of who I was becoming. Now that he had taken that step to ask Jesus into his life and become a Christian, I thought that everything was going to be fine. A couple of weeks later, however, Nick threw a grenade into the centre of our little bubble of joy.

His eldest son had announced he was getting married in December, which by now was only a few weeks away. Nick asked me if I would go with him to the wedding. This was a big ask. His ex-wife, her parents, and the kids would be there. I wasn't too sure that I wanted to go. Nick and I had only known each other for a short time, and I didn't want them to get the wrong impression about me. After all, we had only just met, and he hadn't been in contact with his ex-wife for two years. I said I would think about it. He looked uncomfortable, like there was something else on his mind. I remember he sat on the floor and asked me to sit with him. He took a deep breath.

"There's something you should know before you agree to go to the wedding."

He had a serious look on his face. A wave of fear washed over me.

"What is it?"

The clock sounded incredibly loud, as it ticked its way through the next thirty seconds

"I'm an addict."

There it was, the elephant that had always been in the room. I knew it was all too good to be true. What was he addicted to? I hadn't seen evidence of anything. I couldn't imagine what he was going to say next.

"Donna, I'm a compulsive gambler."

He started at the beginning of the sorry tale, sharing about the addiction that had caused him to lose everything and led him to the streets. There was no trace of self-pity or self-interest as he told his story. He told me, with unflinching honesty, the lengths he had gone to, to fuel his addiction. He had lost his family, his business, his self-respect, and finally, his mind. He told me about his attempted suicides, and lastly, about his admission to a psychiatric hospital. He wanted me to know the whole story before I bumped into any of his family at the wedding - if I decided to go. He didn't want me to hear about his past from anyone else.

Relief! What a relief! Gambling! Not drugs or alcohol. I had been in relationships with addicts of one kind or another all my life. It seemed to me, that on a sliding scale of addictions, gambling came at the very bottom of the heap. It was to be much later I would discover first-hand the true extent of his addiction and the devastation that gambling can cause. Sadly, for both of us, gambling hadn't finished with him yet.

But that day, sitting on the floor in the cottage, I felt reassured, and I wanted to believe that the past was behind him. That day I felt guilty I had forced him to watch the Grand National on TV. Well, doesn't everyone have a flutter on the big races? That day I felt confident i knew how to handle myself around addicts. Five years in Al Anon had taught me to focus on my own behaviour and not on the antics of the addict. I felt that everything was going to be fine. Nick was in recovery and things could only get better. That day, all my reasoning flew away. I was well and truly hooked, already addicted to this man; but somewhere in the back of my brain the warning bell kept on clanging.

I ignored it.

CHAPTER NINE

Two weddings & a lunch

Wedding No 1 - Mark and Emma

I had already met Nick's son Mark and his bride-to-be, Emma. They seemed like a really lovely young couple. Mark was six feet five inches and the image of his Dad. They were both so young, and I admired them for wanting to make such a commitment to one another when so many young, and not-so-young, people were rejecting the idea of marriage and lifelong dedication.

The wedding and reception were to be held in Salford. A few days before the wedding, I started to have worries about attending. Having only known Nick for three months, I hadn't yet met any of his family apart from Mark and Emma. Come to think of it, Nick hadn't met any of his family at that point either. We were both on tenterhooks, wondering how it was going to be on the day. Nick was extremely apprehensive about seeing his ex-wife and in-laws after so long. I was just hoping and praying that we would get through the ceremony without any trouble.

We awoke to a bright, clear, winter's day, with blue skies and sunshine. I chose to wear a bright red embroidered top Looking back, this was not necessarily the best wardrobe choice for the now 'other woman' who had marched into their lives. Nick looked smart in his blue pinstripe suit, courtesy of the ladies in the Monton Age Concern shop. They were continuously on the lookout for second-hand clothes and shoes to fit Nick. Subsequently, he was always immaculately dressed. They say first impressions count, which was why I had been blown away at our first meeting. His sharp clothes and Austin Reed boots hid the fact he was a man living in a halfway house, after living on the streets.

We arrived early, far too early. The weather was quite mild, and my winter red top was much too warm for marching around the streets of Salford. I just kept praying that we wouldn't bump into anyone beforehand. Eventually we went inside. My stomach was churning as we walked into the room full of people. No one came to greet us, so Nick was looking around the room searching for his kids. He saw that one of his sons, with his partner, was stood to the right of the main hall. They had seen us come in, so we made a beeline for them. It was an awkward moment, as they hadn't seen each other for ages, but they welcomed us and told us to stick with them. From the moment we arrived, his ex-wife's family were gathered around her. They looked like they were trying to protect her from any trouble.

Mercifully, the bride, Emma, finally arrived. She looked lovely, and behind her was a very tall, strikingly beautiful girl who was obviously Nick's daughter. He was taken aback at how beautiful his daughter had become. The ceremony was soon over and the taking of the photographs loomed. Nick had his photo taken with the happy couple on his own. Photo call over, we went upstairs where I met Nick's youngest son, who was around nine years old at the time. He was so happy to see his dad. He hugged him like he would never let him go. He hugged me too, which was a lovely surprise. As a bystander, I could feel the hurt in the room. For Nick it was very much a bittersweet day.

We dutifully took our leave of the family members lined up outside the reception room. It had been an ordeal for both of us, but I was glad Nick had been able to be there. As far as I was concerned, we had been present to witness the most important part of the day, the ceremony itself. Inevitably, some uncomfortable and powerful emotions had been stirred up for Nick, which he found difficult to deal with in the coming days and months.

His youngest son was at Mark and Emma's house, sometime after that. We had gone to visit them and he sat between us quite happily, chatting away.

He asked Nick,

"Where do you live Dad?"

"A couple of miles away," Nick replied.

"Oh. They told me you lived miles away."

It was really sad that the kids had no idea where their father was, or how to get hold of him. Nick didn't have any photos of them or, indeed, any photos of his former life. It was as though his whole past had been erased. There had been no-one to advocate for him, or to negotiate supervised visits with his children, when he needed help with that process. I told him I would support him if he wanted to go and seek advice from a solicitor about access to the children. Sadly, despite numerous attempts, we were left with no alternative but to stop legal proceedings. This all had severe consequences for Nick and his children's future together. We are thankful that his relationship with Mark and Emma has remained strong to this day.

Wedding No 2 - Holly and Ryan

Holly and Ryan were a young couple who were members of our church. They were tying the knot in December 2001. It was a lovely wedding. Holly was beautiful in her dress and cape, edged with fur. Everyone was so happy for them and we all wanted to help in any way we could. One of the joys of belonging to our particular church family was the way in which everyone rallied around to help. They had decided to hold an evening reception in a local hall and wanted as many people as possible to join them. It was agreed they would have a potato pie supper in the evening, for friends and family. A number of us said we would make the pies, and supply bread and accompaniments for the feast.

As soon as the ceremony was over, we all set off for an afternoon of pie making, to be delivered in time for the evening celebrations. Together with our friends, Chris and Gill, we set to, and spent the whole afternoon cooking up the filling. Finally, with the pastry on top, it was ready for the oven. It was a huge pie. It was just at that moment that Gill's oven decided not to work. So now we had meat and potatoes, with a raw pastry lid! We resorted to plan B. I lived a minute from their house on the other side of the church. Snow was already falling thick and fast. I remember sprinting across the churchyard with Nick, who was inappropriately dressed in shorts. We opened my oven and tried to shove the pie into it. It was no good - like the ugly sisters' feet and Cinderella's slipper - try as we might, it didn't fit.

Panic-stricken, I rang Adele and Dave, who lived down on the High Street. Thankfully, they had an oven that was large enough and in working order. So off we set with the now well-travelled pie, through the snowy streets of Glossop. Success at last! The pie was in the oven, and was miraculously delivered to the venue on time. Who knew there were so many versions of, and recipes for, the humble meat and potato pie? The whole evening was a fantastic celebration and it got us thinking about our own wedding, which we hadn't announced to anyone, but had been thinking about since we met in Paris, three months earlier.

The Lunch

Nick had obviously met my Mum, when he met me in Paris. He finally met all of my family at Christmas. They took to him straight away. The "big fella", as my Dad called him, was firmly one of the family by the New Year. I had yet to meet Nick's parents and his brother, who lived in Coventry. I was really nervous about meeting them. I don't know why, because I tend to get on with most people.

We duly arrived at his parents' home one Saturday afternoon. Nick's Mum was lovely, very petite and slim. His Dad was pretty much like him, but not so tall. I immediately warmed to Kath, his Mum, and we happily chatted about this and that whilst she busied herself in the kitchen. When all was ready, she called us into the kitchen to help ourselves to the lovely food she had prepared. I helped myself, and she gave me a small tray to carry everything through to the dining room. This was when disaster struck! Somehow, my plate, laden with food and a large dollop of Piccalilli sauce, managed to flip itself off the tray and land face down in the centre of Kath's pale green, plain carpet. The plate was in contact with the carpet for only a millisecond, as I immediately dropped to the floor to pick it up. To my horror, a massive yellow Piccalilli stain covered the centre of the carpet. I heard the collective intake of breath, then silence. Nick spoke first,

"In forty years of being in this house, I have never done that."

He was laughing and trying to make me feel better, but I felt awful. Kath's house was spotless to the point of surgical cleanliness. Despite her protestations that it didn't matter, and it was fine, I knew it really wasn't. For the rest of the afternoon I had to sit and make small talk, whilst the great yellow stain was directly in everyone's eye-line.

Though my first meeting with Nick's Mum and Dad was certainly memorable, I made friends with Kath, and we got on really well over the next couple of years. She had breast cancer, which eventually spread to her bones, and she was often in a lot of pain. The last time she went out into the garden she picked some sweet peas for me, because she knew I loved the scent of the flowers. I was with her for the whole of her final week on this earth, and I cared for her the very best I could.

A lifelong Coventry City supporter and season ticket holder, she had little love for Manchester United, and especially Alex Ferguson, for some reason. Someone had given her his autobiography to read whilst she was bedridden. She told us to take it away or else she would summon up the strength to get out of bed, take it outside and burn it. She had made Nick a promise, when he left for Manchester all those years before, that if he changed his colours and became a Manchester United fan, he would be removed from her will … and she meant it!

Kath's final week was a difficult and emotional seven days. She knew that Nick would now be ok, which gave her some comfort, and a couple of days before she died, she told me that she wanted to ask Jesus into her life, to be her Lord and Saviour. We had briefly talked about faith in the past few months; Kath told me she wanted to ask but didn't know how to, and would I help her. Together we sat and prayed, and Kath allowed Jesus into her life. When she died, we both knew she was going to be alright. She had given her heart to the Lord.

CHAPTER TEN

We nearly didn't get married!

We were still in our lovely little bubble as we went into 2002. Life was great. We met up regularly and spoke to each other every day. I got to know all Nick's colleagues and the ladies in the Monton shop. Nick was getting to know my family and friends in Glossop. It was a really special time of growing in our relationship with one another. We knew we would get married, practically the first week we met, but we thought it was best to wait a while; though we couldn't help thinking that the clock was ticking and we weren't getting any younger. Nick had asked Jesus into his life and was regularly attending church.

Our days were filled with thoughts about the future. Nick wanted to move in straight away and couldn't understand why I didn't want that too. Did I not love him? I did love him, very much, but I knew this relationship had to be different from those that had gone before. I wanted to do things the right way round. In past relationships, I had moved in, or allowed others to move in with me, before I had time to think. It all 'sort of just' happened, and then all 'sort of just' fell apart within a few years. I was tired of revolving-door relationships. Besides, my new-found faith in Jesus was making me see things differently. I didn't want just another relationship. I didn't want to jump into bed with yet another man, even though at times that was a difficult thing to maintain! I wanted a committed marriage with all that entailed. Despite Nick's cajoling, I was holding firm to my ideals. It wasn't easy.

I don't remember Nick asking me to marry him, or him getting down on one knee in a display of romantic fervour. I do remember having a conversation on the way to a Gambler's Anonymous meeting in Manchester, as we walked around the Central Library. We decided, almost at the same time, that we should get married; we loved each other and wanted to be together. That was that. We had the idea firmly planted in our minds. The next stop was to discuss it with Colin, our vicar. Colin was cautious.

> "You haven't known each other very long; I think it would be best for you to wait a while."

I remember saying we weren't twenty somethings who had all the time in the world to wait, that we were in our forties and time was marching on.

Colin took a deep breath.

"When were you thinking of getting married?"

"As soon as we can."

"What about next Easter? I would be happy to marry you then."

Easter seemed a lifetime away. We haggled.

"How about this Christmas"?

He thought for a while, then,

"Okay. I will marry you at Christmas, but first, would you please take

part in a pre-marriage course?"

Of course we would. I would have travelled a thousand miles on bleeding knees if he had asked us to.

Beyond excited, we started making plans. There was only one little detail we had failed to address; we were skint. How could we afford to arrange a wedding? We didn't even have enough for an engagement ring. We would have to think small.

We told our parents about our wedding plans. They both seemed happy for us. Since we couldn't afford an engagement ring, my mum gave me hers to wear, which was so lovely of her. I had decided to make my own wedding dress with Adele. So mum bought me yards of beautiful, ivory silk crepe. I bought a small tiara to wear and a pair of original 1950s gold, stiletto heeled, shoes. Our friends, Chris and Gill, have two children – twins, Bethan and Jack. They were only seven years old and we loved them both dearly. Bethan would be my bridesmaid, and Jack would be the page boy and usher. We bought material for their outfits too. It was going to be a busy few months.

Food was going to be an issue too. We wanted as many people as possible to be able to celebrate with us but, again, money was a factor. One of the women at church, Jan, said that it would be great if we had a 'bring and share' do so that more people could come along. We remembered Holly and Ryan's wedding, and how good it was in the evening. After the suggestion of a 'bring and share' wedding got out, everyone wanted to join in.

We had small groups that met weekly, and each group decided to bring a different type of food. Someone loaned us the use of their vehicle as a wedding car. Vince a member of the church and a dear man said he would take our pictures. The worship team said they would sing, and the deaf-signing group would sign a song, with interpretation in sign language for those who could not hear. Our friends Dave and Adele have a son called

James who made the invites and the orders of service, and also acted as DJ. A lovely lady called Sandra made my bouquet and buttonholes. Another friend, Heather, made the wedding cake. We were overwhelmed by everyone's kindness. The church would be decorated for Christmas, so we didn't even have to buy extra flowers. We decided on the hall above the local library for our reception venue, as it was the biggest space at the time. We arranged we would go there the night before, to dress it up for the following day. The 'big day' was going to be the 21st of December, which was also the shortest day of the year. We would be married at noon, so it wouldn't be too dark to take photographs afterwards. Everything was in place; all we had to do was get ready.

That September, we had to go to London for the day. Or rather I did. I am a member of the Migraine Trust and had been invited to London for a day-long meeting with doctors and other migraineurs. Nick said he wanted to come with me. I explained I would be tied up in meetings for most of the day, but that didn't put him off. He said he would take some time to have a look around his old haunts and then do some sightseeing. We set off from Manchester in high spirits, arriving at Russell Square mid-morning. I headed off to great Ormond Street and Nick went off towards Oxford Street, promising to meet up later that afternoon.

When we finally met up, Nick seemed to be distracted and irritable. I was full of tales about the conference and the research being done into my particular type of migraine. As I prattled on about the day, and the people I had met, I became aware that he was very quiet, so I stopped rabbiting on and asked how his day had been.

He wasn't forthcoming with much information, he just said he had been here and there. Back at Euston bus station, the National Express coach started filling up. Bags, hats, and suitcases were being crammed into overhead racks. The coach heaved a sigh and set off, with its cargo of weary commuters. It had been raining, and as the bodies piled in, water began to evaporate and clung to the windows. It was like sitting in a heavy, wet woollen overcoat. An hour into the journey, conversation was muted; many people were sleeping, bodies slumped and slack-jawed. Nick, who so far had barely uttered a word, suddenly spoke up.

"I've got something to tell you."

"Oh yeah, what's up"?

I wasn't sure I wanted to hear what exactly was up. He took a deep breath.

"I've spent the day in the bookies."

I felt like I had been body slammed to the floor. The physical pain in my gut took my breath away. Then an anger I hadn't felt in years, rose up inside of me. I fought it with every ounce of self-control I could muster. He knew. He knew that by telling me on a crowded, quiet coach, there was no way I would make a scene. Tears welled up in my eyes, I was so hurt. Staring out of the window, fields, and places without names, flashed by me. We were squashed so close together, yet the dreadful silence was huge and deafening. I could feel his heart beating. How could he? How dare he? Where? What on? And the killer question how much? As every ounce of trust I had in him evaporated, I bit my lip hard, willing myself not to cry.

The coach finally stopped in Stevenson Square, Manchester. The passengers spewed out onto the wet pavement and dispersed quickly, like a flock of birds. Rooted to the spot, I watched as the square emptied. The rage that had been simmering in that human soup for the past five hours, exploded into the night air, echoing off the silent buildings, their dark eyes watching us on the pavement below. It all came out at once. I could hear myself shouting, and then screaming at him. What the hell did he think he was doing? I knew it was a mistake for him to come with me. But then, if he had been at home alone, he might have done just the same.

We walked slowly through the streets to Oxford Road. It was late; we went into a fast-food place, which was full of people escaping the cold and the rain. We ordered some food then found a table near the door. Before he had even managed a bite, I slapped my ultimatum on him.

"You can't keep doing this. If we are going to get married, you have got to join a Gamblers Anonymous group. If you don't, we won't have a relationship left."

Nick grasped at that straw I held out to him, with both hands, promising he would go to a meeting that very week. I said I would make sure he did because I would be going with him. Everything had changed. It was the first indication that our little love bubble could be cruelly burst at any moment. Deflated and flat, we sat with our burgers and chips, appetite gone; we forced ourselves to eat. I didn't know how things were going to work out but I was committed to this relationship. We had to make work.

CHAPTER ELEVEN

Married at last

A week before the wedding, everyone was in overdrive. I was making my own wedding dress with the help of my friend Adele. The beautiful, ivory silk crepe, bought by my mum, was cut out on the floor of Adele's huge kitchen. I had also bought some fur to go around the neck and cuffs. The orders of service were ready to go, and a friend, Heather, had made our wedding cake. All the house groups in church had been busy buying, or preparing, whatever they were contributing to the feast. It was a mammoth operation, but everything seemed to be running like clockwork. Then just a few days before the wedding, a mini-disaster struck.

Adele had to go away urgently, and as a result, I was left with the dress which wasn't quite finished. The underskirt and dress needed hemming, but there was so much material that needed to be hand-sewn, I began to think it would never get done. I sat on my bed, picked up my needle and thread, and started to stitch. A few minutes later there was a knock at the front door. Three wonderful women were standing there, needles in hand. Ann, Gill and Hillary came upstairs, climbed on the bed, and started to stitch. It was a scene that could have been taken straight out of 'My Grandmothers Quilt.' The dress was finished with days to spare. I had a pair of original 1950s stiletto shoes and a crystal head band. I was ready to get married. As planned, twins Bethan and Jack featured large in our special day. Bethan was our bridesmaid and Jack our usher. Someone asked me when we knew that we wanted to marry each other. I replied,

"The night we first met."

The night before the wedding we were allowed to go to the hall, to dress it ready for the next day. It was like an episode of 'sixty-minute makeover.' All hands were on deck as we dressed tables and moved furniture. Unfortunately, Nick and I had a massive row because of the stress of it all. But that night, with everything done that could be done, we both went to our separate places to sleep. By this time, my lovely hand-made dress hung on the wardrobe. It was beautiful, not least because of all the love and care which had gone into making it. I had no doubts this time about being married, no worries at the back of my mind. I wanted to marry Nick, and was absolutely sure this was the man that God had chosen for me and who I wanted to be with for the rest of my life. The vows I would make would be solemn and binding, and not taken lightly. I was about to give myself to this man; for better for worse, for richer or poorer, in sickness and health, till we parted at death.

I could not wait.

The twenty first of December dawned with a wintery sun, and a chilly wind blowing. After going to the hairdresser's, I was back at the cottage getting my make-up done and being helped into my dress. My sister Shirley and her husband Adie, along with my gorgeous baby niece Lia, and my Mum and Dad, were all waiting downstairs. As I walked down the stairs everyone was quiet. My Dad looked at me with such love in his eyes, it caught at my heart. Just before noon, everyone, apart from Dad and me walked over to the church, literally a few feet away from my front door. At twelve, there was a knock on the door. A large group of women friends had come to walk me into the church. It was such a lovely thought. My Dad stood surrounded by a throng of women. Although he was a bit startled at first, he didn't seem to mind.

I arrived at the church dead on time. I couldn't really be late as I only lived a stone's throw away. My Dad was busy asking what he had to do. I told him he had to walk me up the aisle, and when Colin the vicar asked, "Who gives this woman to be married to this man? he was to reply, "I do."

"But" remonstrated dad,

"Do I have to say, 'Again,' because I've already done it once before."

The look on my face was enough to tell him that would not be necessary.

I walked into the church and could see Nick waiting for me at the end of the aisle. There were over two hundred people packed into the church, but my eyes were fixed on him. Suddenly it hit me, this was serious stuff. The church was filled with the faces of all those who had loved us and helped us over the years. There were people from Wellington Road, from Gamblers Anonymous, church family and my family. Sadly, apart from his brother Nick's family didn't turn up. His Mum was suffering from terminal cancer, so she stayed at home with his Dad.

It was a sting in the tail, but we were determined not to let it spoil the day. The church was all decorated for Christmas. It was perfect. Our worship team sang and played, and our friend Vince took the photographs. As we faced each other to take our vows, I never meant anything more in the whole of my life. We left the church to a jazzy modern carol, heavy on the saxophone. Outside it was getting colder, and already beginning to get dark, on this shortest day.

We were driven away in a borrowed car and soon arrived at our reception venue, and what a wonderful reception greeted us! So many people, and a banquet fit for royalty. There were hams and beef, dressed salmon, cheeses, and every kind of delicacy you could wish for. The table took up the whole length of the room, groaning under the weight of the feast laid upon it. The ever-versatile James swapped his ushering services for DJ duty. There was lots of dancing, laughter and chatter, as the afternoon merged into the evening. The party ended at 7.00 p.m. giving everyone a chance to get home before the next snowfall. Afterwards, we went to a nearby hotel for a quiet dinner, just the two of us. Then back to a friend's hotel and the honeymoon suite he had gifted us.

It was the perfect end to the perfect day.

Nick: 2003

CHAPTER TWELVE

Nick: 2003

After the hustle and bustle of the wedding and our honeymoon, things quietened down and we got into the routine of living together. It was great at first. Everything was new and we were really happy. We were going out and meeting with friends, and joining in with our church family. I missed my own family very much, and gradually as the year wore on, those feelings of loss and sadness resurfaced. I was starting to feel all the old urges to gamble that I had had before. I was feeling insecure, and although I was attending the church, and meeting with friends, I wasn't comfortable within myself. Our friends, Dave and Adele, left Glossop during that year, which increased the sense of insecurity. We met up with another couple who took over the study group, who were really nice people, but I thought they were very 'clever', and that added to my feelings of inferiority.

I couldn't study the Bible very well. I was never really good at reading. It's only as I have grown older that I realise that I must suffer from dyslexia. I have always found it much easier to listen to something, than to read it in a book or on a screen. Donna didn't seem to have any problems reading or understanding. It says in the Bible that the Holy Spirit gives us gifts, which we can use for the greater good. Donna seemed to have been blessed with more gifts than most. It was hard to admit, but I was just plain jealous of her and our new leaders.

Every time we went to the study group, I would deliberately start a massive argument with Donna before we left the house. By taking all of my anger and frustration out on her, I ensured I would be a picture of calm, leaving Donna in a terrible state for the evening. On top of that, beneath the false image I was giving to others, I was becoming more and more paranoid. I wanted to know where Donna was every minute of the day. I wanted to know who she had been talking to, what they were saying about us, and about me; yet I never ever told Donna my whereabouts if I left the house.

Betting, Buzzing, Breaking

I had been doing some work for my sister-in-law at her house. One day, I decided to pack it in and go to lay a bet somewhere. I decided on Marple. I didn't know anyone there, and it was far enough from Glossop that I was less likely to bump into anyone I knew. Initially, I had a big win. I was back in the zone, buzzing. The old magic was back, but I couldn't leave it at that. I started to gamble there quite regularly. Inevitably, after a week or two, I started to walk away with empty pockets. After this I started to visit a bookies in nearby Hadfield. But Hadfield was riskier because I was more likely to meet someone who knew me there. On the other hand, it was close by, and if I ran out of cash I could easily walk back to Glossop.

I was back on the same old merry-go-round. The more I gambled, the less I cared. All the old behaviour was back with a vengeance. One afternoon I lost a load of money on the 'virtual' dog races. You know you have hit a different level of crazy when you start throwing your money on a bunch of cartoon dogs.

During this mad time, I had been trying to get access to my three youngest children. Time was passing and I hadn't seen any of them. Unfortunately, their mum wasn't answering any of the letters sent to her, including correspondence from the courts. The solicitor was attempting to secure some supervised visits for me, with my children. There was never any response to those requests, nor was there any response to the Child Support Agency. Much later, I discovered that the kids hadn't received many of the birthday cards or Christmas cards I sent to them. The solicitor was getting nowhere with regards to access, and in the end, we reluctantly decided to stop legal action. I don't know exactly how the kids felt about this. I was concerned they would feel like I didn't try hard enough to see them, or support them, but nothing could have been further from the truth. Whilst losing contact with my children, and my parents, was without doubt a major contributor to my depression, it certainly wasn't the whole story.

The postman delivered the mail quite early. This made it easy for me to hide any bills, final demands, or letters from the bank questioning our considerable overdraft. I would rise early so that I could catch him before Donna got up. Whatever was contained in those letters would determine the course of my day. After a while I stopped opening them. I was in free fall.

Increasingly negative thoughts filled my mind and I was unable to concentrate. I became fixated on the fact that Donna still had photographs and letters from past relationships. I couldn't understand why she wanted to keep memories of times which had been so painful and destructive. One night I insisted she destroy any letters or photos from her past. She had been very honest about her life before she met me, and Iwould taunt her with the very private and hurtful things she had told me. I betrayed any trust she still had in me.

Gambling like crazy, one day I walked into a bookies in Glossop town centre and threw my bet on some football match or other. As I left, I noticed someone we both knew walking past. I had no idea if they had seen me or not wracked with nerves, I questioned whether they would tell Donna, or anyone else, that they had seen me.

I would leave home for days at a time, travelling far and wide, to keep gambling. One afternoon in Marple, having won big, I decided I would go over to Sheffield. I knew that I couldn't go back to Belle Vue in Manchester, as I would definitely be recognised. Owlerton Greyhound Stadium was a new place to me. It wasn't far from Hillsborough football ground. I arrived in the afternoon. At the side of the stadium is a large Anglican Church. Ignoring the huge billboard at the front of the church, reminding me that

Jesus died for me, I marched into the stadium and onto the track. I knew that what I was about to do would hurt Donna badly, and probably others including myself, but I couldn't stop myself pressing the self-destruct button.

I arrived with my wages, taken from the house, and spent the rest of the day gambling on everything: horses, dogs and football. The buzz of the stadium, and the adrenaline rush of watching the dogs was exactly as I remembered it, and it all hit me in an instant. At the end of the day, with an empty wallet and only dregs of petrol in the car, I drove out of Sheffield heading for Glossop. I didn't know if I would make it back before the petrol gauge said empty.

It was how I felt.

Empty!

I made it home. As my behaviour was becoming more disturbing and increasingly violent, I could see that Donna was reaching breaking point. Even though I loved her, I couldn't lift myself out of the mess I was creating. I remember that week I went to pawn my wedding ring. I was offered a tenner for the gold band that should have meant so much to me, given what it symbolised. I told the broker to "shove it." The ring stayed firmly on my finger; I hadn't sunk quite that low yet.

Remarkably, Donna was still at home when I got back, and in order to cover my tracks I resorted to being verbally abusive and nasty. I reasoned that if I could start an argument, then I could justify walking out on her. I couldn't cope with her anger and hurt.

Out of control and constantly threatening suicide, I was scary to be around. Donna was so tiny next to me and it was easy to intimidate her. Some days I would drive off in the morning, not returning until days later. When I had been gone for more than forty-eight hours, she would report me as missing. For much of the time, Donna didn't know if I was dead or alive. The constant stress of not knowing where or how I was, or even if I would return, was taking its toll on her mental and physical health. One night, during a particularly bad argument, I threatened to push her down the stairs and spat in her face. It sounds like a cop-out now, to say at times like that I didn't always know what I was saying. Or at least, I knew what I was saying but couldn't stop myself. It felt like I wasn't in control of what was coming out of my mouth. I remember saying I was going to destroy her.

The next day I drove off on one of my sprees. When I arrived home that evening, Donna had changed all the door locks. At first, I was shocked; then I got angry. Banging on the door with my fists, I shouted at her to let me in. I started kicking the front door, not caring who saw or heard me. She refused to open it and told me to go away and sort myself out. I carried on trying to wheedle my way in. Eventually, I gave up. My mind raced. What was I going to do? I went away, returning a few days later on the Sunday morning.

Donna had a friend with her that morning who had been looking after her. She threatened me with the police if I didn't leave. Not knowing what to do next, I turned up at our vicar's house. He took me into his office where I poured out my tale of woe. He waited until I had finished, then launched a tirade at me that I have never forgotten. It didn't seem very vicar-like, but it did the trick. It woke me up to the severity of the situation. He didn't know whether we would get back together and he didn't blame Donna if she threw in the towel. But then he told me that he loved me and gave me some money. He told me I could stay in a bed and breakfast on the High Street, which was owned by Mick, a Christian man who had offered to take me in. I had enough money for two or three nights, to get me off the streets. It was time to start thinking seriously. When the vicar spins you around in his office chair and calls you something unrepeatable, you have to sit up and take notice. I took the money and booked into the B&B.

After a few days I was still without any sort of permanent address. Donna kept in touch with me, as much as I would let her. Everything came to a head one night when I was found on Tesco's car park in Glossop. Donna, and our friend Ann, had been out searching for me. I had left a message to tell Donna I was finally going to end my life. I had no reason to carry on. The police were out searching for me. Donna, Ann, and two police officers crowded around the car. I refused to get out. An ambulance arrived. I didn't want to go to the hospital, but one of the policemen informed me that if I didn't get in the ambulance he would arrest me, and take me to hospital by force. Weighing up my limited options, I decided it was best to go with them.

Arriving at the Accident and Emergency Department, I was seen by a member of the Mental Health Team and a psychiatrist. They asked a few questions and assessed my mental state, then, astonishingly, said I could go home. Problem was - I didn't have a home. Donna was asked if she would allow me to stay the night to make sure I was safe. I held my breath. She said yes. I was told that the mental health team would see me the next day. Donna said I could sleep on the sofa, and then spent a sleepless night herself, watching me like a hawk.

The next day, the people who saw me prescribed a high dose of the anti-depressant, Prozac, to help with the depression, and suggested a course of Cognitive Behavioural Therapy (CBT) to assist with my thought processes and addictive tendencies. I looked a mess, unshaven and unwashed, with crumpled clothes.

Some friends from church, Dave and Ruth, agreed to let me stay with them for a while. They were having some building work done and said that when I was feeling a little better, I could help the builder, as a way of paying for my board. They were so kind to me, but I used to stay in my room much of the time because I didn't want to interfere with their family life too much. They had a son and two daughters, who were great, and didn't seem to mind having me stay in their house.

Donna kept in touch with me every day and accompanied me to see the CBT therapist, named Mark. He was great and really helped us both. I was able to properly look at my thought patterns and my behaviour. I continued to go to church. Donna was going to St. James, so I went to St. Luke's, the other church in our parish. I would sit at the back each Sunday and cry throughout the whole service. During this whole time, unbeknown to us, our friends prayed for our marriage every morning with a picture of us on the table. Two of them had even gone so far as to fast for our marriage. Just knowing that these faithful friends felt so much about us was a blessing as we tried to rebuild our relationship. I do believe that things would have been very different without their love and support. After a few months, I felt that it was time to leave Dave and Ruth's. I didn't want to outstay my welcome. I had already been with them for some time.

I had to find some other accommodation and start sorting my life out. Donna came with me to look at a few properties, but it was really difficult to find anything half decent that would take people who were in receipt of housing benefit with DSS. Eventually I found a flat. Well, it was more like a room, in a house on the outskirts of Glossop. It wasn't great; in fact it was cold and grim looking. It wasn't on any bus route, so I would have to walk into Glossop if I wanted to see anyone. I chose it because I reckoned that when Donna saw it, she would let me come home. My plan backfired. She didn't.

It was the end of November. Donna arrived at my "home" on a dark dreary day. She had bought me a Christmas tree, strung some fairy lights around the bed head and gave me money to put into the heater. One of our friends had brought fresh bedding'. I was devastated that she didn't ask me to leave there immediately! Quite sensibly, she wanted to see some improvement in my efforts to access help and address the gambling, before she would consider reconciliation. Realising she was adamant that I wasn't moving back home at this stage, I settled in for the long haul. I decided it was time to go back to Gamblers Anonymous.

I stayed with Donna over Christmas. One night we talked until the early hours. I had no clue what I was going to do. Who would give me work in the state I was in? She suggested that given God knows what we need, even better than we do ourselves, we should pray for a job. So that's exactly what we did. I must admit I didn't feel hopeful, but Donna had enough faith for both of us.

So we prayed that God would send someone with work for me, and a steady income. I slept little that night wondering what would happen next. We didn't have to wait long. The following morning there was a knock at the door. Peter, a man we knew from church, was standing there. He was straight to the point. He was going to be building a house for the associate minister, next to St. Luke's church, and he needed someone to act as site manager, and that someone was me. I was staggered! God had answered our prayer faster than we thought possible. I didn't know quite what the job entailed but it didn't matter. I had some paid work. Our lives were going to get better.

I started work on the site. I watched as the bulldozer drove in on the first day to start digging the foundations. Over the next few days, I was given instructions to dig a trench where the water pipes were going to go. Despite having been shown what to do, I still couldn't quite work it out. There were two builders on site who started laughing at me. I was furious, so I gave them a colourful mouthful back and stormed off to sit in the car. I could feel the tears of anger stinging my eyes. But then I remembered I had the paperwork that my therapist Mark had given me. It asked questions like, have you done this before? Can you be expected to do a task if you have no experience or training? I realised I couldn't be expected to do something I hadn't had experience of, so I got out of the car and went back to the site. I apologised to the builders for my outburst, and that made them laugh even more. No apologies necessary on a building site. I had to get used to the banter and giving back as good as I got. I realised there had been no malice intended.

I asked again to be shown how to dig the trench, and finally managed to do it perfectly. It was going to be alright. I just had to ask if I didn't know how to do something. As I became more comfortable with the lads I was working with, everything fell into place. We used to go into the church on Thursdays for their coffee morning. I introduced them to cake, and they introduced me to bird watching. Turned out they were real 'twitchers.' I learned a lot from them.

Donna was across the road in the Adult Centre, having signed up for an Access Course. She had always wanted to do a degree in English and she felt this was her opportunity. One afternoon, I was on site with one of the plumbers. We decided it would be fun to throw some of the empty foam canisters onto the fire. We lit the fire and threw them in, one at a time. The noise was deafening. It sounded like a bomb had gone off. Donna was up on the second floor of the building, across from us. A line of faces appeared at the window to see what was causing the explosions. She had the embarrassment of having to admit that one of the "idiots" across the road was, in fact, her husband. Everything was coming together, but I still felt low in mood at times and struggled with abstinence from gambling. Things were much better, but not yet how I wanted them to be. Life was about to take another turn.

Donna: 2003

CHAPTER THIRTEEN

Donna: 2003

After all the excitement of our wedding day and all the good stuff that happened in 2002, we could have been forgiven for thinking that nothing could burst our big, fat, bubble of joy. But as is the way in every fairy tale ever written, I was about to encounter the dark side.

The first few months were exciting and new. We had had a wonderful honeymoon deep in a forest outside York. We spent our first Christmas in a cabin, deep in the woods. It was so secluded it felt like we were the only people on the planet. The smell of pine wood was everywhere; we spent our days walking around the forest looking out for the wildlife. I loved that we could sit in a hot tub underneath a canopy of stars and fresh snowfall. As we hadn't lived together before, we were beginning to get used to being with each other twenty-four seven. We went to York Minster on Christmas Eve, and our friends had bought us tickets to the pantomime Aladdin. We asked people to sign a book so that we would have memories of everywhere we went. Even the owner's dog at the forest cabin where we had stayed, left his paw print on a page. All good things must come to an end however, so we packed up our belongings and headed back to

Glossop to start our life together.

It soon became apparent that Nick was finding it difficult to travel to and from Salford every day. He moved into my tiny cottage, with all his worldly possessions in two black bin bags and a holdall. His six feet two inch frame filled the place. What had been a tiny, cosy space for one, fast became a crowded house. When I bought the cottage, I hadn't even considered the possibility of having to share it with anyone, as I had no intention of being with anyone else ever again. The tiny front room and galley kitchen, which had seemed so spacious when I bought it, was becoming restrictive. When Nick took his shoes off, it felt like they filled the room. In those early days I spent much of my time moving shoes, tripping over shoes and throwing shoes. Come to think of it, nothing much has changed in the shoe department, even now.

Meanwhile, Nick was adjusting to living in a new town, with a new wife and friends, and a fledgling faith. I was still recovering from the stroke but making good progress. I hadn't returned to work so finances were tight, but together we were managing to keep a roof over our heads and pay the bills. Ironically, Nick was much better at managing money than I was. His addiction to gambling had forced him to become a genius at mental arithmetic. He told me he had had to learn fast so that he didn't get ripped off by the bookies. For some crazy reason, I was more than happy to let him take care of our finances. It was a very bad move.

Initially all was well. Nick was attending Gamblers Anonymous regularly; and I attended Gam Anon. It became a lifeline for me, meeting with other people who had been through, or were still going through, the nightmare of having a family member or friend addicted to gambling. I listened wide eyed to the stories the people told in those rooms each week. So far, Nick was managing to keep away from gambling, but our lives were about to unravel.

He was missing his kids desperately. I would often wake in the early hours to the sound of him crying. He was devastated at the thought he might never see them again. He never tried to downplay the impact his addiction and associated behaviour had had on his first marriage and on his kids. On the contrary, he was brutally honest about the things he had said and done.

I felt so sorry for him, and for his family. Whilst I acknowledged that his behaviour had been unacceptable, and downright dangerous at times, I also felt that he should have been given at the very least, supervised access to his kids. Unfortunately, neither his social worker nor mental health team had been able to broker any sort of compromise with his ex-wife. I knew that the last time he had seen the kids alone, was soon after he had come out of hospital for the final time. It had been a disaster, as he was way too emotional and fragile to be left alone with them. Much later we spoke to his ex-wife about it, and she told us she had made the decision not to let the younger children see him again because of the affect it had on them. That decision, which she made purely to protect her kids, had unforeseen consequences further down the line.

We went to see a solicitor soon after we married, to see if we could get at least some access to the kids. Despite our best efforts, the solicitor's efforts, and even the court's efforts, Nick never got to see the them again. His eldest son continued to see him and became the only link he had to the rest of his family. After many months of going backwards and forwards to the solicitor, Nick decided it was probably best, for his kids, to leave things as they were. I didn't agree but had to stop pushing the issue. Nick hoped that as they got older, they would come looking for him. His eldest son continued to see him and still has a strong bond with his Dad to this day. It was probably a little easier for him to see his Dad as a person, rather than an addict, as he was older when Nick was forced to leave the family behind. He also got to see first-hand, the change in his Dad as time went on.

In the January, Nick's eldest son and his wife had a baby boy. We decided to go to Hope Hospital to see him. It was so lovely to see the new baby, Nick was a proud grandad.

Gambling Again?

I suspected that Nick had started gambling again. Initially, I couldn't put my finger on anything specific. He started leaving the house early, before I got up, and was vague about where he had been, when he returned home. I was uneasy, but without any evidence of wrongdoing I kept my fears to myself. When he had briefly returned to gambling before we married, I had insisted he go to G.A. if we were to continue the relationship. At that time, it seemed to nip it in the bud. I was noticing he was skipping meetings, but I reasoned that life was getting busy for us both. With so many distractions, it became difficult to keep track of his movements.

One afternoon he came home and informed me he had given in his notice at Age Concern. Trouble was - he didn't have another job lined up - and because he had walked out of his job, he didn't qualify for unemployment benefit. I was furious. As everyone knows, burying your head in the sand is a stupid strategy for dealing with problems. By the time our problem surfaced, it had become a HUGE issue and was already well on its way to taking over every area of our lives. Meanwhile, Nick was becoming more defensive, more depressed, and controlling of my own behaviour and whereabouts. He would either be very withdrawn and silent, or aggressive, loud and argumentative. There was no middle ground. He no longer wanted to go out with friends. If we did happen to go out for an evening, he would provoke an argument before we left home so that I would arrive feeling anxious and longing for the evening to end. He wore a mask of normality to everyone else.

After a short time of unemployment Nick decided he would like to work for himself. The only question was, what to do? I was glad he was at least talking about work, as we were really struggling to make ends meet. Then one evening he announced out of the blue,

"I want to be a gardener, but I don't want to work for someone else."

He didn't feel he would be able to do it alone, so asked if I would be willing to help him. I had a million reservations and didn't really feel that I wanted to be a gardener, but we needed the money and jobs were thin on the ground. So, gardening it was.

Once we made the decision, we were blessed that friends gave us work. We took it very seriously, even enrolling on a horticulture course to increase our knowledge of all things horticultural. Out of everything we learned on that very informative course, the one thing we both remembered the most was the definition of "perching", or the perched water table. This fascinating bit of information stood out for some reason. Perching is when water lies on the top layer of soil but doesn't seep down to the lower layers. It can happen when the soil is very dry and unable to absorb surface water. A kind of metaphor for what happens when you don't deal with things. It all looks fine on the surface, but beneath, it is dry and lifeless.

Eventually we built up a small, but regular, client base. Word of mouth brought us even more clients. We were gifted a second-hand car which helped us to transport equipment, along with a few resident spiders. Nick's mood improved and he took great pride in his work, but two perfectionists working together was a recipe for disaster, at least on the gardening front. Every blade of grass was lovingly clipped, and every flower border meticulously weeded and made perfect. We took too long over each job and asked too little in the way of payment. As the bills rolled in, we needed to take on more work to make ends meet.

Gardening is a great way to exercise and improve your mood. Getting out in nature, a perfect antidote to stress and depression. But at first, we found the physical work difficult. Added to that, we hadn't really thought about what we would do for income over the winter months. A number of our gardening clients were happy to give us cleaning jobs, so that's what we did. As the winter closed in, we started to clean houses instead of gardening. We worked long hours, travelling further afield to pick up work. Eventually, the travelling and the physical work took its toll on me physically, and Nick's mental health was starting to suffer too. He started cancelling jobs and staying at home. I was frantic. We had a diary full of commitments and no way of fulfilling them. As I didn't drive, I couldn't just take off on my own.

The atmosphere at home was becoming heavy and dark. When Nick did feel up to it, we would work all day in silence. Some days I spent alone, walking long distances between jobs in order to honour our commitments. The cracks in our relationship were opening up. I felt totally powerless to prevent us from sliding into the chasm opening up before us. He insisted it was my entire fault he had got into this situation, and I wore my guilt like a heavy cape on my shoulders. I couldn't talk to anyone about what was happening at first, because I was so ashamed. My big fairy-tale relationship was fast becoming worse than my worst nightmare. I wasn't ready, or able, to confess that everything was going wrong.

I had to account for every minute I was out of the house: where I had been, who I had spoken to and what I had said. Nick even made it difficult for me to leave the house at all. He was constantly threatening to leave me, and finally the threats of suicide weighed heavy on my very soul. I became afraid to leave him for any length of time in case he harmed himself. I was fast becoming the fearful, co-dependent person I had struggled so hard to get away from. It was obvious, at least to me, that Nick was mentally ill, but he refused to seek medical assistance and didn't want me to seek help myself.

Powerless, and robbed of any self-confidence, my world started to contract. I stopped seeing friends or speaking to family, afraid they might ask too many questions. Outside the house I put on a mask of normality, to hide the state of the chaos in our relationship. I was good at this; I had had lots of practice in my previous relationships. I couldn't bear the thought of people pitying me or gossiping about me. But despite my best efforts, I was finding it more and more difficult to hide the mess that our lives had become. My nerves were shredded, and if I started to talk for any length of time, I burst into tears. It felt like there was a brick lodged in the centre of my chest where my heart should be. I ached.

One sunny Friday morning, Nick took all the cash I had hidden in the house – it was a week's wages. He climbed into the car, gave a cheery wave goodbye and drove off. It was midsummer and exceptionally hot. I tried to continue working alone, but without transport it was heavy going and exhausting. Walking everywhere, often in tears because I was so scared; not knowing what had happened to him consumed my thoughts, always imagining the worst. He could have been at the bottom of a ravine for all I knew. Three days later he would show up, full of remorse. He wouldn't tell me where he had been, only that he had slept in the car for the past three nights. I felt physically sick. Here was this man I had tied myself to, who was abusing me financially and emotionally. I didn't have a clue what to do about it, except pray. I was so angry at God for bringing us together. Even angrier that the vows I made on our wedding day were serious and binding. At least to me they were.

The disappearances became more frequent. Nick would return dishevelled and uncommunicative. I lost count of how many times I had to contact the police, who put him on their missing persons' list. Often before he left, he would threaten to commit suicide. Knowing his past history I felt that these were very real and credible threats, which left me sick with worry. He was seriously mentally ill but still refused to see our doctor.

Drowning in Debt

After each of these disappearances I would be relieved to see him walk through the door, glad that he was at least alive. As time went on, that relief turned into fear of him coming home, and then a rage so deep I had to fight every single day to keep it under control. Towards the end of the year he was out of control and gambling heavily. He stole money from the house and from my purse. He was using credit cards, which he had newly acquired, which he maxed up to their limits. He had emptied our bank account and the overdraft was up to its limit. The debt was now piling up. Bills went unpaid. Final demands, and threatening letters, thudded onto the doormat with alarming regularity. In the past, Nick had tried to hide any post, now he didn't care. I wasn't eating. I didn't have enough money to buy food, so I existed on toast and jam. The debt was now a huge mountain that neither of us could ignore. The bailiffs soon followed.

Trapped in a marriage with a seriously ill and out of control husband, I tried to carry on. Nick's finger was firmly on the self-destruct button. He spent his days driving around, gambling and sleeping in the car. All the old behaviours were back with a vengeance. Now doing the work of two people, I was burnt out and losing grip on reality.

There was a menacing aspect to Nick's behaviour. He would say the most vicious things, and although he never hit me, the threat of violence was always there. My little life was crashing down around me. I was past caring for myself. I was crying openly in the street and had stopped taking care of my appearance. My hair was ragged as I couldn't afford to get it cut. I was losing weight at an alarming rate, not eating or sleeping. I was on the verge of a mental breakdown myself. Depression hung over me and I could no longer hide what was happening; I was way past caring what others might think of me. At other times I would hide away, not answering the phone and refusing to see anyone.

Sometime later, Nick's mental health workers said that the most distressing thing for them was watching the impact it had on my mental health and well-being. Very sad, and now very afraid of this beautiful man I had married, I would walk home at the end of the day filled with trepidation about what I would find on the other side of the front door. I finally caved in and started to confide in close friends. They immediately rallied around me, listening, praying and giving sound advice. It helped that people now knew exactly what the problem was.

We were drowning in debt. When the bailiffs came knocking, I would sit on the stairs, shouting at them to go away. The mortgage hadn't been paid for months; we were on the verge of financial collapse and repossession of the house, which I had tried so hard to keep going. Nick was now sliding deeper into depression. I was on my knees praying that something would change. Our G.P., Nicola, was so sympathetic, but made it very clear that unless Nick wanted the help, we couldn't force it upon him.

The 'Filofax Incident'

Mental illness in a loved one can be terrifying, when you don't understand someone's behaviour or the way they are thinking. One particular night, Nick was shouting at me, wanting to know where I had been and what I had been saying about him. He was totally paranoid. Finally I snapped. Picking up the coffee table I hurled it at the wall, and then started throwing anything I could get my hands on. Not satisfied with this, and out of control, I started to kick and punch him. Finally I picked up my Filofax and threw it at him. It skimmed the top of his head. It wouldn't have hurt him but it did make him angrier.

The house looked like a tornado had just ripped through it. Broken crockery and furniture covered the floor. All the hurt and rage I felt came spewing out of me, as I slammed doors, screamed louder, and threw anything I could break, at the wall. It has gone down in our history as 'The Filofax Incident.' We can laugh about the absurdity of it now, but I still remember the desperation and the terrible pain I felt at the time. I was barely functioning, feeling worthless, and clueless as to what to do next. But as I kept reacting to Nick's behaviour, which, by the way, I knew was the wrong strategy, the more he seemed to take delight in seeing me get angry.

Some people started telling me that no one would blame me if I walked away from the marriage. I took legal advice about my rights, and Nick's rights, should we divorce. Summer was coming to an end; I wasn't sleeping and had started having suicidal thoughts myself. A voice kept telling me I was a waste of space, that I was the common denominator in all my failed relationships, and this was the last straw. I was starting to believe the voices. It was true.

I started to believe I was condemned to live alone because I was ugly, stupid and worthless. I walked everywhere with my head bowed, I didn't dare look up in case I saw someone I knew. I didn't want to have to talk to anyone or see the concerned look on their faces. Some people I knew were actively avoiding me and would cross over to the other side of the road if they saw me coming. I didn't blame them. Yet, in spite of all the pain and the madness, I could still hear another voice - a small, quiet voice - telling me to hang in there, all would be well. It was the same reassuring voice I had heard years before telling me to go to St. Luke's. It was a voice I trusted, because I just knew it was the voice of God. Despite this reassurance, I had to finally admit defeat, and realise I had to let someone close enough to help me. I called my friend Tracey.

When she arrived at my door, I must have looked dreadful. She came in, sat me down and packed a bag for me. Completely worn out, I didn't protest. Closed in on myself, I had no tears and no words. I let her carry on. Once she had all the essentials, she gently took my hand and led me out of the house like a little child. I stayed with Tracey for the rest of that week. She and Steve, her husband, were so kind to me.

I still had to work out how to keep working. I let all the gardening jobs go and just concentrated on the cleaning jobs. The problem was, we normally did them together, and now that I was on my own it was taking me twice as long to do the same job. The summer was long gone, and leaves were falling off the trees. Normally I would be delighted by the changing season, but now I just walked with my head down, not looking up at the trees or the sky. I had just finished a job and was walking back to town. It was a clear, crisp day, and as I walked along, the leaves on the pavement gathered around my feet making a crunching sound. Reaching the High Street, everything started to blur, I realised I was crying. Not caring who heard me, I cried out,

"Jesus, please help me!"

No sooner were the words out of my mouth than I was stopped in my tracks. What seemed like five feet ahead of me on the pavement, was a man. I saw Him nailed to a large oak tree covered in leaves and branches. Blood poured out of Him onto the leaves, the bark and the ground. I could see myself curled up at the foot of the tree, completely covered in blood – His blood. It was so graphic and so gruesome, like a movie being played out in front of my eyes. The man on the tree I recognised was Jesus. His head was covered in a skull cap of thorns. The cross beam nailed to a living tree was not like the traditional crosses you see in pictures. Pain, agony and deep sadness were etched on His face. I huddled close to Him, shocked, yet feeling protected. I had never experienced anything like it. Then I heard His voice,

> "He wants to destroy you, but he can't have you because you are mine."

To my left, a grotesque being was trapped inside a cage glaring at me. It held onto the bars rattling them in frustration. It was so startling and so powerful. I don't know how long I stood there. It seemed like ages. Then, the vision faded. As it did, a moment of complete clarity came to me. All that was happening to me, to us, was demonic. Nick was in the grip of something evil, set on destroying both of us. I remembered then that Nick had used those words himself.

One evening, some weeks earlier, Nick was being particularly irrational and abusive. I was at the top of the stairs outside our bedroom. Nick threatened to push me down the stairs. He spat in my face and said he was going to destroy me. Much later I spoke to Nick about this incident. He said he didn't remember saying or doing that to me. He said that sometimes he knew what he was saying, and other times it was as though someone else was speaking. I prayed and prayed, and just kept getting a picture of us with a crimson ribbon wrapped around our wrists, binding us together with Jesus.

A verse in the Bible kept coming to me, *"A person standing alone can be attacked and defeated but two can stand back to back and conquer. Three are even better, for a triple braided cord is not easily broken."* *(Ecclesiastes 4: 9-12)*

Despite these comforting words and the visions of Jesus, I was struggling to see a future for Nick and I. Concerned friends and family were starting to question the wisdom of us staying together. If I had been outside of our relationship, looking in, I might have said the same. No matter what, leaving did not seem the right course of action to me. I knew we had to stay together come what may, but I couldn't continue living in the same space; my nerves were completely frayed.

After much soul searching, I came to a horrible decision. Nick was behaving bizarrely and had gone missing yet again. I decided to change the locks on the doors. I could no longer cope with the worry; I was totally exhausted. I needed rest and space. Something needed to happen, to break the vicious circle we were caught up in. That night when Nick arrived home, he tried to open the door, and when he could not gain entry, he shouted to me to open the door. I was terrified, and worried about disturbing the neighbours' late at night, but I remained determined. He begged me to open the door. My heart was breaking and I was really scared. I told him, through the locked door, that I needed him to go away, to get his act together. He needed to seek help from the doctors and the addiction groups. I told him I loved him so much; that I wanted us to be together, but right now I couldn't have him living with me. Eventually he walked away. Relieved, I sank to the floor and howled.

The tears I shed at that time could have filled a lake. I had forgotten how to smile and how to laugh. One evening as I was talking to God in prayer, I experienced another vision, and saw a large, circular pool filled with crystal clear water, set in the middle of a beautiful garden. He told me that these were all the tears I had ever shed. He had seen and captured every one of them. I realised in that moment that He knew me, really knew me. He knew everything I was going through, had been through and would go through in the future. I don't know how I got through that night. I know I shed even more tears to add to that pool, but I know He saw every single one of them.

Desperately worried about Nick, where he would go and what he would do, I sat terrified, thinking that having been backed into a corner, he might finally take his own life. I felt I had abandoned him, but it was the only way to get some space to think. Over the next twenty-four hours I fretted that he might come back, and in a fit of anger he might break the door down. I thought it might be best if I wasn't there, so I went to my sister's house a few miles away. He wasn't likely to come looking for me there. I had heard on the grapevine that Nick had stayed with friends, Tim and Abi, over in Stockport. At least I knew he was off the streets and safe. In a terribly fragile and emotional state, I cried easily and didn't sleep much. It still felt like a huge brick was lodged in the centre of my chest. My heart literally ached. Later I discovered that Nick had moved in with some friends in Glossop, but would soon need to look for a place of his own.

"Talk of the Devil …"

When I heard the clear, deep voice telling me it was going to push me down the stairs and destroy me, I froze. But then suddenly everything clicked into place. I had heard that voice before; in my past, it used to tell me to go and hang myself. I hadn't heard it for some time, but now that it had announced itself, I knew exactly what to do. After months and months of emotional abuse, mental torture and deep sadness, all the hurt and terrible physical and emotional pain - that 'voice' gave the game away. I finally knew what to do next, who and what I was dealing with, and how to get rid of it.

The atmosphere in the house was oppressive, as though a fog had completely filled the place. The stairway felt dangerous every time I climbed it. I could sense the presence of something evil and I had come to the end of my patience with all this nonsense, it was time to take control and fight back. I had heard a lot in church, and read in the Bible, about the authority that Jesus had. You might be thinking it was okay for Him, because He is the Son of God after all, but let me share something with you that might surprise you.

After Jesus' resurrection, and just before His ascension when He left the earth, the Lord Jesus gave the Great Commission to His apostles and said that all authority in heaven and on earth had been given to Him, and He was passing that same authority on to His apostles (see Matthew 28:18-20). Through the Great Commission, the Church has received that same authority. In the same way that a police officer has a position of delegated authority, from which to exercise and enforce the law, so too, a Christian who is filled with the Holy Spirit has delegated spiritual authority from Christ, over demons. So that day, I took the authority given to me in Christ. I spoke loudly and clearly to the 'voice.' I commanded that spirit to leave my house in the name of Jesus. Then I opened every window and walked around the whole house, claiming it back for Jesus. I put on worship music and sang my head off for two hours solid.

I stopped, turned off the music and listened. Silence! Absolute silence! The cottage felt quiet and peaceful. For the first time in months, I let out a long sigh of relief. I asked the Holy Spirit to fill the house with His presence and peace, and He did.

I am not denying the reality of mental illness, not at all. In both my own past and in Nick's, we had each suffered in different ways from the effects of depression and anxiety. On the lead-up to the incident of the stairs, and the ensuing exorcism from my home of the 'voice,' we were under enormous pressure, and the circumstances were taking their toll on our emotional, physical and mental health. However, there was a further dynamic to what was happening that I am endeavouring to describe, this was on a spiritual level. I am not suggesting that every mental health issue is demonic. Neither am I saying that this voice was a figment of my imagination. I believe that the voice was that of an evil spirit, and when I prayed, God heard my prayer and the authority of Christ cleansed that demonic influence from my home. I prayed this way because I have a deep faith in Jesus. Otherwise, I would never have taken this course of action.

I felt for Nick, that there was some spiritual sickness within him, but his primary focus had to be on seeking medical help first. Depression is a complex, isolating illness. At the chemical level, it is an imbalance of chemicals within the brain. You cannot see it happening with your physical eyes. What you see and feel are the feelings of loneliness, isolation and worthlessness that depression brings with it. The inability of others to understand the experience of true depression, is a part of what makes it so isolating. The most dangerous factor is a person's deep sense of hopelessness. Someone without hope is the likeliest candidate for suicide. Hope can't be given on prescription, but it is essential for good mental health. We cannot survive without hope of better things to come.

Nick was given medication, and prescribed treatment at that time, which undoubtedly helped him. I am not denying Nick needed medical intervention, but there were also other darker elements to our situation. Whether you are able to accept it or not, I believe there was a spiritual entity, which could not be cured by drugs, only God could deal with this type of situation and give us true hope for the future.

Nick: 2004

CHAPTER FOURTEEN

Nick: 2004

Summer was well under way and I was still suffering from depression. Prozac didn't seem to be helping massively, although I have to admit I don't know what I would have been like had I not been taking it. Donna and I were still not back living together, but we were working on our relationship and things were beginning to reconcile.

We had decided we would go to Detling, in Kent, to a Christian Conference being held there. I had only been to a similar conference once before in Skegness, called Spring Harvest. This was much bigger and I wasn't sure about what the programme would be. We set off from Glossop early in the morning, but our old, battered car had broken down just outside Oxford. We waited ages for the recovery vehicle to reach us. It was so frustrating to be stood on the hard shoulder only a few miles away from our destination. The recovery man took one look at the radiator and read the last rites over it. There was nothing for it; we had to make the decision to go all the way back to Glossop on the breakdown truck. So it was that we arrived back home around 10.00 p.m. that night, exhausted and with no idea what to do next.

The next morning, Donna said that she really felt we should still go and suggested we could hire a car. We decided to do just that, but we prayed, asking God to help us sort it out because we couldn't really afford to hire a car. We finally arrived in Detling the following afternoon, twenty-four hours late. We wasted no time in pitching our tent and getting to know the people camping around us. Looking at the itinerary I wasn't too sure about the list of workshops, but went to the main tent for the evening celebration.

On the first, full day there, Donna said that she fancied going to a seminar entitled, "Praying with Fire," being led by two ministers, Catherine Brown and Arnold Muwonge. I was distinctly uncomfortable, and felt agitated and a bit afraid of what it was all about. I told her I didn't want to go. Donna said that was fine. I could stay at the camp and she would go alone. I didn't want to go but I didn't want to stay either. In the end I decided to go with her, under the condition I could sit at the back so that I could leave if I needed to.

We arrived at the marquee, which quickly filled with people. Around four hundred people were gathered in there. Outside, it was a hot, August afternoon and the sun shone bright in a clear blue sky; the air was still, with not even a breath of wind. The sides of the marquee had to be opened near the front to allow whatever air was out there to circulate. Catherine Brown, a tiny Glaswegian minister, and a Ugandan pastor called Arnold

Muwonge walked into the marquee, they were both really joyful. They said they had been praying before the session and felt that God was going to heal people that day.

They invited everyone to start to pray, and as people prayed, an actual wind started to blow around the tent, which got stronger and stronger. The sides of the tent were blowing outwards and the roof of the tent was moving up and down. The woman in front of me fell backwards into my arms and I realised that a number of people were now lying on the floor. My first instinct was to get out of there, and fast. Instead, I was compelled to go forward when Catherine asked people to come up for prayer. I set off to the front of the queue like a greyhound out of the traps!

When I reached Catherine, she asked me my name. She laid hands on my head and started to pray. She said that Jesus wanted to heal me of my depression and my addiction to gambling. I was amazed. I hadn't told her anything about my addiction or depression. What happened next was even more astonishing. She spoke these words over me,

"Nick, be healed in the name of Jesus."

I felt myself falling. I saw a bright, white light before I hit the ground. As I lay there, unable to move, something lifted off me like a heavy overcoat. I lay on the floor for some time. It was as though I was held there. I could hear everything going on around me, as others were being healed by this amazing presence. Eventually I was able to get up off the floor, stunned and amazed at what had just happened to me. I felt fantastic.

As we approached our tent back at the camp, a really funny guy from Northern Ireland, called Phil, came towards me. He proceeded to tell me that he thought God had given him a picture for me. In the past, I would have been walking fast in the opposite direction, but after what had just happened, I was all ears, eager to hear what God had to say. In his own inimitable Northern Irish accent, Phil told me,

"God has had you in a fire blanket for a very long time and as you   came into the camp, I saw that monkey jump off your back."

He asked if anything he had said made any sense to me. My mind went straight back to that awful night in Buile Hill Park where I had sat with the petrol can and cigarette lighter, intent on setting myself alight. A fire blanket made absolute sense to me.

I felt totally free for the first time in years.

We arrived home from Detling, absolutely buzzing. As we opened the front door, there on the mat was a cheque, for just over the amount we had spent on hiring the car. We could scarcely believe it. Our prayers had been answered again. It was the first of many blessings which came our way over the next few months. I was feeling better than I had done for years. From the moment that Catherine prayed for me, I had felt free and light, with no hint of the heaviness and depression that had dogged me for so long.

I made a decision.

Stopping the Prozac anti-depressant tablets was the only way of knowing if I had been truly healed. Generally speaking, it is not advisable that anyone should stop their medication abruptly without consulting their doctor, especially not anti-depressants. I wouldn't encourage anyone to do what I did. However, I was so sure that Jesus had completely healed me, and the only way for me to test it out was to stop taking the tablets. I didn't tell my doctor, or Donna, what I was doing. I truly believed that whatever had happened in that tent was something supernatural from God and that the Holy Spirit had healed me.

Two weeks after we came home, I had an appointment with my doctor. The conversation went something like this:

Doctor, "How are you, Nick? How is the medication suiting you?"

Me, "What medication?"

Doctor, "What do you mean?"

Me, "I've stopped taking the tablets. I've been healed."

Doctor, raising her voice slightly, "What do you mean you've been   healed?"

I told her what had happened. She told me how poorly I had been. She stressed how much the doctors and the mental health team had been trying to help me. How much trouble and pain I had caused Donna. She gave me a real dressing down. I just kept repeating,

"But I feel fantastic, I feel really well."

She asked if I had been gambling.

"No."

She asked me how my mood was on a scale from one to ten. I replied,

"Definitely an eight or a nine."

She was obviously concerned that I might relapse, and concerned for Donna's well-being and how this would impact on her. She asked me to make an appointment at reception, for a couple of weeks' time. She would review my situation again. In the meantime, if my mood deteriorated, I was told I must make an urgent appointment. **I never needed to make that call.**

Praying for the Sick

It was a really hot August. The work on the church house continued. Every Thursday, there was a coffee morning at St. Luke's, next door. I called in to get a coffee and cake for myself and the builders. Whilst I was in the church, I saw a woman wearing a surgical neck collar. I felt a really strong urge to pray for healing for her. I couldn't do it in the church because I felt too embarrassed. I pottered about outside the front of the house until she came out. As she drew level with me I stepped forward, clearing my throat.

"Hi. I'm sorry to bother you. I can see that you have something wrong with your neck. I feel that God wants me to pray for you."

She looked startled but was open to me praying for her. I prayed a very simple prayer.

"In the name of Jesus, be healed."
That was it.

She hugged me and thanked me, then went on her way. I went back to work on the house. Later that night, our friend Laurie phoned, to tell me that the lady I had prayed for had gone home, taken her neck collar off and was pain free. She even decided to clean the windows, with no ill effects! She was overjoyed. It was a real miracle for her to be pain-free, after years of suffering. The effects of her healing continued. I was amazed that God had used me to heal someone. It was yet more evidence of God's power at work in me and around me. My faith grew massively as I saw first-hand that Jesus was not only able, but also willing, to heal many of the people I prayed for.

The house build was drawing to a close. Donna and I had met every day in that house as it went up, eating lunch together and talking about the future. I had learned a lot about myself in the past few months. I was growing in confidence. I had even managed to climb the ladders up to the apex of the roof - something I couldn't even have dreamed of doing just six short months before. I was still well mentally, but I was worrying a little about what I would do when the house was completed. Donna was almost at the end of her course and preparing to go to university. We were spending much more time together. I was staying at home more, and we were attending Gamblers Anonymous every week. Autumn came and went, with nothing on the horizon. I should have known better; God was still very much on the case.

Something came back to me about a saying in the Twelve Step rooms,

"God didn't drag you out of the water just to kick you to death on the beach!"

Donna: 2004

CHAPTER FIFTEEN

Donna: 2004

Nick and I were gradually rebuilding our relationship, albeit we were still living apart. We decided to go to a Christian Conference at Detling, in Kent. I had been once before, a couple of years earlier. Nick was quite low in mood, and despite taking large doses of Prozac each day, his suicidal thoughts had increased in frequency, causing him to become agitated and paranoid. Ironically one of the side effects of Prozac can be suicidal thoughts. I really wanted to go to the conference to get a break from the constant stress and worry, and to spend some time with God. Convincing Nick and myself that it was a good idea, I booked two places. Two friends of ours, Jan and Alan, were also going, so we agreed to meet them there. Yet, how could I ensure that Nick wouldn't back out at the last minute. His mood was so unpredictable, and it was difficult to make any plans as they could be scuppered at the last minute. Emotionally, I was walking on broken glass and so very tired.

It was a beautiful summer morning and everything seemed hopeful. We loaded the camping gear into our battered, old estate car. It moved and sounded like an armoured tank setting off on its last campaign. So far, it had been okay driving around town, although it did need lots of encouragement to get it up the hills around Glossop. I have to admit I did have my doubts that it would get us to Kent in one piece. Nevertheless, we set of very early that morning, heading south.

The sheer volume of traffic on the roads to the M1 was horrendous. Despite being cool when we set off, the day was morphing into a hot August afternoon. We chugged along, finally reaching the M40 just outside Oxford at around lunchtime. The noise from the car's engine was deafening; the car could take no more of the heat, or the mileage. We came to a grinding halt, amidst a slow-moving snake of metal and rubber creeping along the motorway tarmac.

At first, we saw what looked like wisps of vapour coming from beneath the bonnet. Then, alarmingly, large clouds of red-hot steam poured out, obstructing our view through the windscreen. Frantic, but thankfully in the inside lane, we pulled onto the hard shoulder. Cars drove by with their occupants craning their necks to see what the matter was, and no doubt assessing the risk to themselves as they drew alongside us, in the event of the petrol tank deciding to blow itself to pieces! Neither of us knew anything about cars or mechanics, but we both knew the radiator was in trouble. Mercifully we had breakdown insurance, which I had convinced Nick to take out only the week before. We rang the company and the nice man at the other end of the line assured us they would get to us ... eventually.

The huge traffic jams on the motorway network, meant it could be hours before they were able to reach us. Lots of stricken vehicles were dotted along the hard shoulders, blocking emergency vehicles and recovery services from reaching people quickly. We reluctantly got out of our pressure cooker of a car and climbed behind the crash barrier as instructed. We settled in for a long wait. It grew cold at the roadside, despite the high temperatures elsewhere. Hundreds of cars rumbled past us as the summery morning deteriorated into a chilly afternoon. We were both cold, thirsty and exhausted by the time the breakdown vehicle reached us more than four hours later.

The mechanic peered under the car bonnet and pronounced the radiator to be "terminal." We had a choice; we could continue on our way to our destination in the hope that someone, somewhere, could fix the car, but that seemed highly unlikely, or we could turn around and head back North. We were within minutes of Oxford, but couldn't risk being stranded between there and Detling. Reluctantly, we decided to go home.

The driver of the breakdown vehicle was lovely. He drove us to the nearest service station and told us to take our time, and to get something hot to eat and drink. I ordered a bowl of tomato soup, which I proceeded to tip down the front of my new, white t-shirt. Ever after known as 'the day of the soup meltdown,' it was the final straw. I burst into tears in the middle of the crowded service station and bawled my head off like a baby. Nick was beside himself with embarrassment at my very public display of emotion. He kept hissing at me to stop crying, which just made me cry all the more loudly.

Still hungry, and now wet, with a huge orange stain on my once pristine t-shirt, I climbed wearily into the cab of the lorry. The driver looked concerned but at least he didn't laugh. The journey back took ages and there was little conversation. We arrived back in Glossop late that evening, right back where we had started some fourteen hours earlier. Despite the horrendous day we had had, I still really felt we should go to the conference. The problem was how to get there? We decided that the next morning we would hire a car; we would pay for it on the credit card and really pray that God would come up with the money for it. We told Him. Yes we told the Creator of the Universe what to do!

"If You want us to go, You will have to find the money to cover the cost of the car-hire because we can't afford it."

We awoke the next morning in a hopeful mood. We picked up our lovely new hire car, loaded all our gear and set off again. This time the journey was much less stressful. For one thing, we were confident the car would get us to our destination. Mid-afternoon, we finally arrived at the Kent County Showground. We quickly pitched our tent. Having already lost a day, I was keen to get to as many things as possible. Nick seemed less enthusiastic. That first night we went into the main auditorium. I could see that Nick was distinctly uncomfortable. A few thousand people were worshipping together, praising God with their arms raised in the air. Some were even dancing. We sat right at the very back, near the exit, so Nick could get out quickly if he needed to. After the celebration we met our fellow campers. One of the guys was a Northern Irish man, called Phil, who was hysterically funny and kept us all entertained for the rest of the evening. The next morning Nick awoke in a morose mood. He was adamant he didn't want to go to anything that day. I was torn between leaving him behind and going on my own. In the end I decided to go on my own to some of the sessions. I realised that whilst I was busy focusing on Nick and his behaviour, it was taking my focus away from the real reason we were there; to meet with God. I went off with a heavy heart. I spent the rest of the day just soaking up the atmosphere. I was beginning to feel much more relaxed and peaceful. God was most definitely at work. That evening I returned to our tent. I could see Nick, sitting at the front opening of the tent. The awning was flapping in the breeze and He looked like a Bedouin traveler sitting there, all alone, with the setting sun behind him. We awoke the next day to blue skies and warm sunshine. That afternoon, a Scottish minister called Catherine Brown, and a Ugandan minister, Arnold Muwonge, were hosting a session called,

"Praying with Fire." It was all about encouraging us to pray, inviting the Holy Spirit to come to minister to us. There was the problem right there, as far as Nick was concerned. He had a real hang up about the Holy Spirit and all the "supernatural" stuff. To Christians, the Holy Spirit is the third person of the Trinity. God is One God in three divine Persons: God the Father, God the Son and God the Holy Spirit. When Jesus left the earth, He promised that the Father would send a comforter, the Holy Spirit, who would remain with us, and fill us with His power and love. Acts 2 in the New Testament of the Bible describes that power, and the way in which the Holy Spirit came to empower the first disciples. I felt nervous. Nick wasn't too keen to go to the session. Problem was, he wasn't keen for me to go either. Finally I told him that he could come along and sit near the back of the marquee, but I was definitely not going to miss the opportunity to encounter the Holy Spirit. I realise that what I am saying here, and what happened next, might test the faith of many Christians, let alone any non- Christians reading this, but this is a true account of what happened that day. Nick decided to come. When we arrived at the marquee, four hundred people were already there, waiting for the session to begin. Outside it was a hot, sunny August day, with a clear blue sky and not a breath of wind. As the day wore on, the temperature rose higher. Catherine and Arnold finally arrived, laughing and talking. They both had a lovely way of speaking. There was no drama or shouting; they were clear and calm and full of joy. They explained what they were about to do - they were going to invite the Holy Spirit to come in power, and they expected that many people would be healed that day and set free from addictive behaviours. They called us to pray, and to call on the Holy Spirit to move in power. The noise level rose as four hundred people raised their voices in prayer. A sudden wind started to blow around the marquee. It swirled around, becoming stronger. As it became stronger, the roof started to move up and down, and the side walls of the marquee began to move in and out. People started to fall over spontaneously; it became really difficult to stay on your feet as the wind grew stronger. A lady in front of us fell backwards into Nick's arms. People were laughing with joy and absolute amazement at what was happening. Catherine started to call people forward for prayer and healing. To my shock and surprise, Nick started to walk to the front of the marquee. I followed him. There was a long queue of people waiting patiently. All around us, people were lying on the floor, seemingly pinned there by some powerful force. Many people were on their knees crying and only a few were standing upright. Nick finally made it to the front of the queue. Catherine, who was tiny, lifted her hand over Nick and she spoke with authority. She asked his name then said,

> "Nick, God wants to heal you of your depression and your gambling addiction. Be healed in the name of Jesus."

Nick hadn't told her what he suffered from or what he was addicted to. He hit the floor like a felled tree. I was standing with a group of people, as I watched Nick fall. Arnold spoke over us, and we all fell to the floor as a powerful wave hit us full on. I can't begin to describe it, or how it actually felt. It was beautiful, awesome, delicious, and scary, all at the same time. You just couldn't stand up under the weight of the presence of God. I lay on the floor in that tent. Stunned at what had happened but amazed at the awesomeness of God.

We arrived back at the camp, both of us in a state of bliss and shock, knowing that we had just met with something, Someone amazingly powerful. As we arrived at the camp, Phil came up to us and told Nick that he believed God had been telling him that the monkey had jumped off his back, and that God had had him in a fire blanket for years. He asked if it meant anything to Nick. Absolutely! From the moment he was rescued in the park (after covering himself in petrol on Millennium night), it seemed that God had had His hand on him. It just confirmed what had happened in the tent. We were amazed. It proved to us both that this was real. God was real.

We returned home that weekend. Opening the door, we saw there was an envelope on the carpet. I had long had a fear of unknown post coming through the door. This looked particularly ominous. It had 'Her Majesties Revenue' written all over it. Did we owe tax now? I thought we had better open it; I had stopped avoiding bad news. But no, God had done it again. Inside the envelope was a cheque for an amount that was twenty pounds more than we had prayed for to cover the costs of the hire car. We had been awarded a tax rebate. It was completely out of the blue. We hadn't applied for it or sought it in any way, yet there it was. We didn't need any more confirmation that God really was working in our lives.

Nick hadn't told me he had stopped taking his anti-depression medication, but he seemed remarkably well and happy.

Summer was drawing to a close and Nick's work on the house would soon come to an end. I had watched the house build, as it rose up from the foundations. Like the house, we both felt that our marriage was being rebuilt from the ruins. We still lived apart but saw each other every day and at weekends. We were getting along better than ever.

As the build came to a close, I have to admit we did wonder where Nick's next job would come from. I had almost completed my access course, and had learned a lot about myself over those past nine months too. Recovering well from the stroke, I was improving day by day. Studying was helping me to function better. I had wanted to study for a Degree in English for years and now it seemed that everything was finally falling into place.

Now that the building work had finished, Nick found himself alone at the site. Most days he painted indoors, or turned the soil in the garden ready for shrubs and plants to be bedded out. We had become accustomed to meeting for lunch there and had come to look on it as our place. Somewhere we could be alone and get to know each other better. It was reassuring that I could see Nick from the classroom window in the Adult Education Centre. Unfortunately, I could also hear him. One day, he and one of the other lads, who had come to complete some work, thought it would be amusing to throw empty canisters of expanding foam onto the fire in the brazier. The noise was beyond loud. It sounded as though a bomb had gone off. The explosion echoed around the streets nearby. The whole of my study group ran to the windows to see what had happened. Having to explain to my startled tutor that the "idiots" making the noise were not only known to me but I was also married to one of them, was not my finest moment.

Whilst we were at the conference in Detling, Catherine Brown had prayed for me and told me that she felt God was saying I was a 'seer'. A seer is someone who can "see" things that others can't see, in the natural realm. She felt that God was going to use me to give pictures and words to people, and for myself. Since coming back home, I had been regularly seeing pictures as I was praying for myself and others. In the past, my focus had been on "seeing" spirits, and mediumship. Now God had taken that sensitivity and started to use it for His purposes; to speak into people's lives. I still see pictures. At other times it is like watching a film playing out in front of me. I know it sounds crazy, but believe me, they are very clear, and always relevant and very specific.

As I was praying one morning, I saw Jesus standing between me and Nick. He had wrapped a scarlet cord around our wrists and bound us together. Then He wrapped the cord around His own wrists. It once again brought to mind, the verse in the Bible that talks about the three stranded cord not being easily broken.

"A person standing alone can be attacked and defeated but two standing together can conquer. Three are even better for a triple braided cord is not easily broken."
(Ecclesiastes 4:12)

It was a late summers evening. The sun was disappearing behind the trees, casting a pink glow over the garden. I was sitting with Nick, talking about our future. We could not see where the next step would come from. I had my heart set on university and Nick needed some paid work. I truly believed that just as God had found work for Nick in the past, He wasn't about to let Him down now. The build had come to an end and the keys had been handed over to the vicar. It felt strange that we wouldn't be able to just walk into the house whenever we pleased. It was a bittersweet moment for both of us.

As we didn't quite know what to do next, we just waited. Within a few days we were invited to a friend's house for dinner. We were supposedly there to watch a football match but we should have known better.

The Master was about to make His move.

The Jericho Project

CHAPTER SIXTEEN

The Jericho Project

The Jericho Project was birthed out of a desire to serve the community in Glossopdale, Derbyshire, and to give employment opportunities to local people. It involved three local churches – St. John's in Charlesworth, the Bishop Geoffrey Allen Centre in Gamesley, and Holy Trinity church in Dinting, besides local councillors, the Community Voluntary Service (CVS), and other voluntary bodies. A furniture project was set up, as was the Jericho Cafe on Gamesley, a social housing estate on the edge of Glossop.

A friend of ours, Tim, sat on the committee overseeing the café, which had been closed for a while. It had been losing money and was not proving viable as a business at that time. One evening he invited us to his home to watch a Coventry City football match. Tim and his family supported Scunthorpe United, so there was always some friendly rivalry and banter. Avid Coventry fans, we couldn't afford to go to all the matches, so we were really pleased to have been invited.

Whilst we were there, Tim said there was something he wanted to talk to us about. He produced a booklet, which contained the results of a survey carried out with the local residents of Gamesley. The majority of those asked, had expressed a desire to see the cafe reopened. It was meant to be a Christian outreach to the community. The committee was in the process of relaunching the cafe and advertising for a manager to run the project. The manager would be responsible for the day-to-day running of the cafe and would manage a team of volunteers. Ideally, he or she needed to be sympathetic to the Christian ethos of the project. Having given us the preamble, which we politely listened to without comment, Tim delivered the killer blow,

"I believe that God is telling me, Nick, that you are the man for the job."

Nick's response was swift.

"Not a chance. I had my own business and I ran it into the ground through gambling. I don't want to run, or be in any way responsible for, another business. I do not want the responsibility of having to account for money, or be involved in financial management in any way."

Tim listened patiently to Nick's refusal speech but was insistent that Nick was the man. As a team, he felt the two of us would be perfect. Now it was my turn to raise objections. I was going to university, so wouldn't have time to help Nick in the café, or anywhere else for that matter. Tim just smiled at us both, and asked us to go away and at least think and pray about it. He handed us the survey. We had a lot of thinking and praying to do. Yes, Nick needed a job, but he didn't want to jump at the first thing offered to him, it had to be the right move. We both told Tim we would think about it. As far as I was concerned, I had already thought about it, and I wasn't about to change my mind. In the weeks that followed, we prayed and talked and prayed some more. We asked our friends for prayer and advice regarding a way forward. We needed to be sure that this was the right thing to do, because it would take a lot of hard work and commitment. I had no catering experience whatsoever, and although Nick had run his own business, he had not been involved in the catering side of things. In those days of seeking for answers and some sort of guidance, one Bible verse kept on jumping out at us,

"Feed my sheep," from Chapter 21 of the Gospel according to John.

Jesus' words to His disciples started to crop up all over the place. Random people would come up to us with those very words from Chapter 21 of St. John's Gospel, not sure why they had to tell us to do that. We started to be given sheep; not real ones, but knitted and pottery sheep, and Bible references to sheep. It was crazy. One Sunday, we found ourselves over in Tilsley, in a small Baptist church. We sat on the front row. That evening an old Welsh preacher had come to speak. He was very tall, with grey hair and a bushy beard. He was leaning on what looked like a staff or a shepherd's crook. Suddenly, in the middle of his talk, he mentioned Chapter 21 in John's Gospel. Turning to us, he pointed the stick straight at us, saying in a loud voice,

"Jesus says to you, 'Feed My SHEEP.'"

We both fell about laughing. If we had had any doubts about what we were being asked to do, they were finally dispelled. God now had our undivided attention. We were about to set out on an adventure that neither of us could have dreamed or imagined. We didn't have any connection with Gamesley. In fact, we had never been there. It had developed into a large housing estate, established in the late 1960s around the heart of the original village. Many of the people who came to live there were originally from East Manchester and Salford. The first people to arrive found themselves in the middle of a large building site in the middle of farmland. Paths and roads had not yet been laid at that time. It was, and still is, a beautiful part of Derbyshire, surrounded by hills dotted with sheep. There are remains of a Roman fortification called Melandra Castle, the foundations of which are still there. There was very little else. Without shops or transport, it must have seemed like they had landed in the middle of nowhere.

Today there are around 1,500 houses, about a third of which are privately owned. There is a primary school, a nursery, a doctor's surgery, a church, a library, a row of shops, and an infrequent bus service. So far so good, but did we really want to work in a community we knew nothing about? We read and re-read the survey Tim had given us. The more we read it, the more excited we became.

One morning Nick announced,

"We need to go and look at the place."

"Are you sure? I mean you always said you didn't want to run another business and I will be going to university soon."

Nick sucked in a deep breath.

"I couldn't do it without you, Donna. It's got to be both of us. I couldn't run it on my own."

Now it was my turn for the deep intake of breath. I wasn't sure about putting my own plans on the back-burner for the foreseeable future. I really wanted to take a degree in English and Creative Writing, and now, I wasn't sure how I felt about giving up my dream.

"Let's go and at least look at it" he said.

Nick seemed more animated than I had seen him in ages. So, we arranged to take a look at the cafe in the place we had never been to. It was a gloomy, wet day, not the best day to go looking at properties. Still, if we thought it was okay on such a horrible day, it could only get better, right? We arrived late morning and a lady called Ann let us into the building. She opened the shutters, unlocked the door and said she would leave us to have a look around. Switching on the lights we surveyed the scene. The worn, grey-tiled floor was covered in splodges of bright yellow paint. The Community Payback Team had been hard at work painting everything in sight. The unit was much larger than we expected, with a kitchen at the far end. The centre of the room was dominated by a huge tower of tables and chairs, which almost reached to the ceiling. The kitchen was somewhat tired looking, with old wooden units and an ancient domestic sink. A domestic four-ring gas cooker was attached to one wall. Outside, a concrete canopy ran the length of the row of shops, preventing any natural daylight from getting into the building, which added to the gloomy interior. We looked around and then at each other.

"I love it!" Both of us shouted almost simultaneously.

We didn't know why, but this place was immediately tugging at our hearts. I was already thinking about how it could be made brighter and more inviting. There was one small problem, neither of us was a trained chef; we had trouble cooking for more than two people. How on earth were we ever going to be able to cook for lots of people. Pushing the rising panic to one side, there was no doubt we were hooked, but what to do next? We left the café, and Ann, promising we would go away and think about it. She handed us an application form and a job description. We waved goodbye and set off into the wintery wilds of Gamesley. We walked up the Mews, with its row of shops and a pub, then around the edge of the estate, taking in the surroundings. We were surprised by what we saw. God was letting His love for the people of Gamesley wash over us, as we walked around Jericho.   We got the job. That is, Nick got the job, and I came on board as a full-time volunteer and trustee. I gave up my dreams of creative writing and have never looked back. We have been in the community for over sixteen years now and so much has happened in that time. Tim was right. Nick was, and is, the right man for the job. We were made a charity ten years ago and have continued to serve the community of Gamesley and beyond. At the heart of all we do, is the desire to share the Gospel and the love of Jesus, and to "Feed His Sheep."

In Conclusion; our hearts go out to anyone who is suffering, especially from addiction or mental illness, and to their families and friends who suffer along with them. As time went by, all the pain and anguish faded for Nick and me. As I write this, we are so thankful for the opportunity to take all of our failures of the past and look at them with the fresh eyes of overcomers. Our pasts have become the story which can help those who are now suffering, as we did. There are long standing consequences to our decisions, made many years ago, but slowly, the hurts and regrets are being turned into positives.

It is good to remember where we came from and the astonishing things that God has done in our lives. He took two extremely damaged individuals, brought them together, and through the power of His Spirit and the love of His people, He has loved us into wholeness. He can do that for you too. If you are reading this, be in no doubt that what He has done for us, He surely can do for you if you will let Him. With the help of our Father God and the sacrificial love of Jesus, we have been rescued, carried, healed and provided for. We know who we are now in Christ. We have security and know that we are valued. By the grace of God our marriage remains strong. We have supported each other through sickness and difficult times, which still come. We are not immune from the struggles of life on this earth, but our difficult times have been eased knowing that Jesus is in the boat with us. He is capable of calming any storm and carrying us through it to the other side.

We are blessed with the love and support of family and friends. Over the past few years Nick has been in contact with some of his children and grandchildren and the healing and restoration in his family is still ongoing.

It is a world away from the situation we found ourselves in when we first met. We praise God, because we have so much to be thankful for. We were once like dust being blown around by the wind, living in pain, fear and captivity.

NOW WE ARE SET FREE!

Thank You!

Thank you for reading our story. We hope that it has blessed you and opened your eyes. For those still struggling with addiction or who have friends or family in the same situation you will find further sources of help in the following pages.

If you feel that you want to ask Jesus into your life as we did then say the following few words. We guarantee He can and will transform your life, you will not regret it.

Lord Jesus Christ, I am sorry for the things I have done wrong in my life. I ask your forgiveness and now turn from everything which I know is wrong. Thank you for dying on the cross for me to set me free from my sins. Please come into my life and fill me with your Holy Spirit and be with me forever.
Thank you Lord Jesus. Amen .

In the Book of John in the Bible it says
For God so loved the world that he gave His only son that whoever might believe in Him shall not die but will have eternal life
John. Chapter3 verse 16
If you have asked Jesus into your life then tell someone close to you. Look for a church that you can join that will help you to understand and grow in your new faith. We wish you well.

GLOSSARY OF TERMS

Bending the dog - an illegal and cruel practice of manipulating the dog's performance by overfeeding, over exercising or drugging the animal to slow it down. The handicappers will then give it a more favourable position at the start of the next race so that it has a better chance of winning.

Traps - the name given to an enclosed starting gate used in greyhound racing.

Pegs - the trackside bookmakers boards where they take bets.

Middle Distance Stayers Race - a race over 450 to 550 metres.

Off the pace - dogs which race behind the lead dog and come from behind strongly at the   finish.

A short head - the smallest measurement that a dog can win by.

Eclampsia - a condition in which one or more convulsions occur in a pregnant woman. It is characterised by high blood pressure, often followed by coma, and causing a threat to the health of mother or baby.

Anorexia Nervosa - an eating disorder in which an individual restricts food intake leading to significant weight loss. Accompanied by an intense fear of gaining weight or becoming fat even when underweight. It causes a disturbance in the way in which the individual views or denies the seriousness of their low body weight. It can affect people of all ages, sexual orientation, gender or race.

Glandular fever - An infectious viral disease characterised by swelling of the lymph glands, fever sore throat and lethargy. It is caused by the

Epstein Barr Virus, one of the most common human viruses. It used to be known as the "Kissing Disease," as it can be passed between individuals.

M.E. Myalgic Encephalomyelitis - Is a serious neuro-immune condition characterised by malaise, a reduction in functioning and a severe worsening of symptoms after even minimal exertion or concentration. It causes dysregulation of the immune, nervous and energy metabolism systems, it is also known as CFS or Chronic Fatigue Syndrome.

H.I.V. - The Human Immunodeficiency Viruses are two species of Lentivirus that infect humans. Over time they cause Acquired Immunodeficiency Syndrome, a condition in which progressive failure of the immune system allows life threatening opportunistic infections and cancers to thrive.

Co-dependency - in a relationship, is a behavioural condition where one person enables another person's addiction, poor mental health, immaturity, irresponsibility or under-achievement. Signs of co-dependency include difficulty making decisions, difficulty identifying your feelings, difficulty in communicating in a relationship. Valuing the approval of others more than you value yourself. Lacking trust in yourself and having low self-esteem.

Al Anon/AlaTeen - Al Anon Family Groups are there for families and friends of alcoholics, who share their experience, strength and hope in order to solve their common problems. There are meetings throughout the U.K. and worldwide.

Twelve Steps of Al Anon - these are adopted almost word for word from the Twelve Steps of Alcoholics Anonymous and have been a tool for spiritual growth for millions of members. At meetings, members share the lessons they have learned as they put the Twelve Steps into action. You do not have to have a specific faith in any deity or belief system to use the Twelve Steps.

Y2K bug - this was a computer flaw or bug that could have caused problems when dealing with dates beyond December 31st, 1999. Instead of 4 digits, many computer programmes at the time allowed only two digits e.g. 99 instead of 1999. This meant that when the year changed to 2000 the digits 00 would have caused havoc as computers worldwide stopped working on the 31st of December 1999.

Hemiplegic Migraine (H.M.) - a rare disorder in which affected individuals experience migraine aura which can affect vision, speech, sensation and mental ability, along with one sided weakness or temporary paralysis. It may or may not be genetic

Transient Ischaemic Attack (T.I.A.) - a brief episode of neurological dysfunction resulting from the interruption in blood flow to the brain or eye. Sometimes prior to a stroke.

Alpha Course - Alpha began at Holy Trinity Brompton/HTB in London in 1977. It was attended by Nicky Gumbel in 1990 who made it into a course for those outside of the Church. It was created to be used by local churches focusing on the essentials of Christian faith common to all denominations. Alpha is now worldwide and has been translated into 112 languages; it has continued to be used by the Church as a means of sharing the Gospel of Jesus.

Prozac - Fluoxetine sold as Prozac is a type of anti-depressant known as a serotonin re uptake inhibitor (SSRi.) It is often used to treat major depressive disorder.

Cognitive Behavioural Therapy (C.B.T.) - is a talking therapy, which can help you to manage your problems by changing the way you think and behave. It is most commonly used to treat depression and anxiety.

APPENDIX 1

SIGNS OF PROBLEM GAMBLING

People who gamble compulsively often have substance misuse problems, personality disorder or anxiety problems. A compulsive (or pathological gambler} is unable to resist his or her impulses. This can lead to severe consequences for themselves and their families. For people who fall into this category, the urge to have a bet is so great it can only be relieved by gambling, until the problem is identified and help sought. There is now compelling evidence that the reward system in the brain is activated when gambling, in the same way as when taking drugs or alcohol.

The signs include:

Spending more than you can afford on gambling.

Difficulty stopping or regulating your gambling.

Thinking of or talking about gambling even when you are not 'in action.'

Lying, being secretive and hiding evidence of gambling - like betting slips.

Having or starting arguments with family or friends about money or gambling.

Losing interest in usual activities or hobbies.

You have borrowed money or sold things to get money to gamble.

You think you may have a problem.

Your gambling has caused health problems including depression, stress and anxiety.

Other people have criticised your gambling, even if you think you don't have a problem.

Your gambling has caused financial problems for you, your household or friends.

You have felt guilty about the way you gamble and its consequences.

You have chased losses to get out of financial trouble.

You gamble until all your money is gone.

You have borrowed money and possessions, or not paid bills, in order to pay for your gambling habit.

You need to gamble with larger amounts of money, or for longer periods, to get the same feeling of excitement or buzz.

You neglect work, school or family, your personal needs or household responsibilities, because of gambling.

You feel anxious, worried, guilty, depressed or irritable.

You had, or currently suffer from, depression as a result of your addiction to gambling.

You isolate yourself socially.

You are mentally or emotionally abusive to those closest to you.

You have lost relationships, jobs or properties as a result of gambling.

You are now presently homeless, or have been in the past, on the streets or in a hostel, as a result of losing your job or your home.

You have spent time in prison or court as a result of your gambling.

ORGANISATIONS & CONTACT INFORMATION

Action for M.E. UK
www.actionforme.org.uk
Tel:01179279551 Mon-Fri 9am-5pm

Alpha UK
www.alpha.org.uk

Childline UK
Tel:08001111

Christians Against Poverty
Free debt counselling www.cap.org.uk
Tel:01274760720
New   enquiries helpline Tel:08003280006
contact@cap.uk CAP Money Courses/CAP Release Groups.

Citizens Advice UK
www.citizensadvice.org.uk
Adviceline (England) Tel:03444111444
Adviceline (Wales) Tel:03444772020
Textphone 1800103444111445 9am-5pm Mon-Fri

Cognitive Behavioural Therapy NHS
www.nhs.uk

Cruse Bereavement Care
Free phone Tel:0808808167

GamAnon UK and Ireland

www.gamanon.org.uk

NSO Secretary nsosec@gamanon.org,uk

GamBan

Blocks access to thousands of gambling websites on all devices

www.gamban.com

Gamblers Anonymous (G.A.)

National tel:03300940322

North East tel:07771427429

North West tel:07974668999

Ulster tel:(028)71351329

info@gamblersanonymous.org.uk

Gambling With Lives

For families bereaved by gambling related suicide

Tel:07864299158

info@gamblingwithlives.org

GamFam

Run by parents of compulsive gamblers

www.gamfam.co.uk

GAMSTOP

Gambling Self Exclusion Scheme

www.gamstop.co.uk

Tel:08001386518 8pm until 12 midnight 7 days a week

Healthy Minds

Tel:01865901600

Migraine Action
www.migraine.org.uk/contactus/
Tel:08456011033 + Facebook

Migraine Matters
www.migraine-matters.com + Facebook

MIND
www.mind.org.uk

National Debt Helpline UK
Tel:01613595528

National Problem Gambling Clinic
Specialist help for those aged 13-25. You can self-refer to this service.
www.gambling.cnwl@nhs.net
Tel:02073817722

Refuge Domestic Abuse Helpline
Tel:08082000247

Samaritans
Free phone 116123

SANEline
Tel:03003047000 4.30pm-10.30pm daily

Survivors of Bereavement by Suicide SOBS
National Helpline Tel:03001115065 9am-9pm Mon-Fri

The M.E. Association

Helpline Tel:03445765326 10am-12md, 2pm-4pm, 7pm-9pm daily
admin@meassociation.org.uk

The Migraine Trust

Helplines open 10am-4pm Tues and Thurs Tel:02039510150
Telephone lines open Mon-Fri 10am-4pm Tel:02039510150

The Mix for Under 25s

Tel:08088084994
Sun-Fri2pm-11pm

The National Gambling Helpline

Tel:08088020133

The Stroke Association

Helpline tel:03033033100
helpline@stroke.org.uk
Textphone:1800103033033100 + Facebook, Twitter

YGAM

The Young Gamers and Gamblers Education Trust
hello@ygam.org
Tel:02038374963

Connect on Facebook, Twitter Instagram and You Tube

About the author

Donna is a retired nurse, midwife and lecturer in midwifery. She lives in the Peak District with her husband Nick

Nick is the manager of Café Jericho, a Community Café outreach and registered charity in Gamesley, near Glossop. It is staffed by a number of volunteers who give their time to serve the community.

Donna is a full time volunteer in the Café and a trustee of the charity.

They both follow Coventry City Football Club along with some of their children and grandchildren.

They have a deep love for Jesus, and a passion to see people saved, set free and healed from addiction and all kinds of physical, mental and spiritual sickness.

Contact Info:

donnarogers.dr.58@gmail.com

www.donnarogers.co.uk

Donna can also be found on Twitter and Facebook @donnarogers

Café Jericho is a registered charity, 6 Winster Mews Gamesley

DerbyshireSK13 5EZ

It can be found on Facebook

Printed in Great Britain
by Amazon

13077462R00136